DATE DUE

PRACTICAL SAMPLING

Applied Social Research Methods Series
Volume 21

APPLIED SOCIAL RESEARCH METHODS SERIES

Series Editor:
LEONARD BICKMAN, Peabody College, Vanderbilt University, Nashville
Series Associate Editor:
DEBRA J. ROG, Vanderbilt University, Washington, DC

PRACTICAL SAMPLING

Gary T. Henry

Applied Social Research Methods Series
Volume 21

SAGE PUBLICATIONS
The International Professional Publishers
Newbury Park   London   New Delhi

For information address:

SAGE Publications, Inc.
2111 West Hillcrest Drive
Newbury Park, California 91320

SAGE Publications Ltd.
28 Banner Street
London EC1Y 8QE
England

SAGE Publications India Pvt. Ltd.
M-32 Market
Greater Kailash I
New Delhi 100 048 India

Printed in the United States of America

Library of Congress Cataloging-in-Publication Data

Henry, Gary T.
    Practical sampling / Gary T. Henry.
        p.   cm. — (Applied social research methods series; v. 21)
    Includes bibliographical references (p.
    ISBN 0-8039-2958-7. — ISBN 0-8039-2959-5 (pbk.)
    1. Sampling (Statistics)   2. Social surveys.   I. Title.
II. Series.
HA31.2.H46   1990
300'.723—dc20   90-8240
                                                                    CIP

FIRST PRINTING, 1990
Sage Production Editor: Astrid Virding

Contents

Acknowledgments

Practical Sampling would not exist without the contributions and support of many individuals. Mary Stutzman, Seymour Sudman, and Greg Rest provided me with useful reviews. The series coeditors, Leonard Bickman and Debra Rog, were encouraging and diplomatically requiring. Kent Dickey and Virginia Hettinger gave the text, formulas, and calculations a painstaking review. Tim Hendrick and Pat Storino polished the graphics. Sue Mahan and Annie Kurtz took my diskettes and scribbled notes and gave me back clean, printed chapters. Kathy Reynolds never begrudged the weekends that I spent writing rather than repairing the failing porch, and Amy Wray, my daughter, never doubted that the book would be finished.

1

Introduction

Most data used in the social and policy sciences are collected from samples. Public opinion surveys, social experiments, and evaluations of educational innovations are examples of research where sampling is routinely used. In any research in which the findings are being extrapolated from the subjects or units under study to a larger study population, sampling is being utilized. Samples are so frequently utilized that counterexamples—studies where the entire study population is involved, such as the decennial U.S. census—are relatively rare. Without relying on sampling as the basis for collecting evaluative data, the risk and cost involved with adopting new methods of teaching or social service delivery would be difficult to justify. Evaluating the effectiveness of new programs would be prohibitive.

The introduction and use of probability sampling techniques have stimulated the growth of empirical social and policy research in the later 20th century. Despite the importance of sampling, researchers in the social and policy sciences receive little practice with sampling and often seek guidance concerning practial sampling applications. Assumptions about sampling methods often underlie analytical techniques that the researchers wish to utilize. Researchers often need to insure that the assumptions are justified.

The sampling dilemma is simple. Time and cost prohibit a researcher from collecting data on the entire group or population that is of interest for a particular study. However, researchers and the consumers of research are usually interested in the population rather than a subset of the population. Extending the study findings from a subset of the population, or ''sample,'' to the entire population is critically important to overcome the dilemma between cost and time on the one hand and information needs on the other. Knowledge of basic sampling logic and methods is fundamental to ascertain if study findings reasonably apply to the population represented by the study participants or the survey respondents.

Understanding sampling and its implications is especially important in policy research. Questions that commonly arise in conducting and using policy research directly related to understanding the choices made in sample design are: Is the target population for the policy or program defined in the same way as the population in the study? Have the methods for selecting the subjects or units biased the estimates needed by policymakers? Are estimates from the sample data precise enough for the study purpose? Table 1.1 highlights these three issues, the criteria used to make judgments about the usefulness of the study, and the potential implications for using the study results.

Using an example of an assessment of service needs for the advanced elderly, the impact of sampling design choices on the results can be shown:

- *Population definition.* A study is to provide a service needs assessment for all advanced elderly in a state. If the population from which the sample is drawn is current clients of publicly provided social and medical services, then elderly not being served but who need services are excluded. This choice would produce an underestimate of actual needs.

- *Sampling methods.* A sampling strategy that focuses on elderly living in group residences could bias the results. Group residences provide the highest level of care in many instances. Therefore, the estimate of needs, when extrapolated to the entire elderly population of the state, may be too high. The sample would not include enough self-sufficient elderly living on their own or with family members.

- *Precision of the estimate.* An estimate, say a mean or proportion, produced from a sample, even when the sampling method is unbiased, is subject to fluctuation. An uninformed consumer of the study results may assume that an estimate is exact and place too much credence in the "exact" estimate. For instance, an estimate from the needs assessment may indicate that 63.4% of the advanced elderly require service. For a small sample, the researcher may be reasonably confident the true mean is between 54% and 73%. Assuming 500,000 advanced elderly in the population, the estimate of the service population varies by nearly 100,000 from one end of the range to the other. In this case, the estimate may be too imprecise to establish policies and programs for service delivery to the advanced elderly.

SAMPLE DEFINED

The word "sample" is used in a variety of ways in scientific and everyday language. For example, Mark and Workman (1987, p. 47) point out that, "To the chemist, the word sample conjures up the image of a small pile of something, or perhaps a small container of liquid, paste, or maybe 'gunk,' of which the composition must be determined." The sample is intrinsically important to the chemist. It may be all of the substance that was available, for instance from a crime scene, or part of a larger mass that has been selected. But determining the composition of the sample is an end in itself. Discovery of arsenic in the tea is the forensic chemist's charge, not a representation of the population of tea.

TABLE 1.1
Issues in Sample Design for Policy Research

Issue	Criterion	Implication
Population Definition	Consistency of target population and study population	Study population yields biased results by including members not in target population or leaving out members who are in target population
Sampling Method	Sample selection equally likely to select any member of study population	Sampling methods yield biased results if some study population members are more likely to be selected than others
Precision of Estimate	Estimate precise enough to inform policy decision	All samples yield estimates, not exact figures. Lack of precision can impact on the decisions to be made

The chemist's sample can be classified as a specimen, where the particular case is important. In contrast, sample, as it is used in the research literature and in this book, means a subset of the population that is used to gain information about the entire population. A sample in this sense is a model of the population. A good sample will represent the population well. The sample does not have intrinsic interest to the social or policy scientist: it is a tool to find out about the population.

Two questions arise naturally from this discussion:

- How should one select a sample that will be used to represent the population?
- How do we judge whether the sample represents the population well?

Guidance concerning the first question will be addressed in the next chapter and continued throughout the book. In Chapter 3, possible sources of error in the sample and a framework for making choices in the sample design process are presented.

Before turning to these discussions, a comment on the use of the word "represent" is germane. A sample is used to represent the population. Thus, it is a model or representation of the population. Adding the term "representative" to "sample," as in the commonly used phrase "representative sample," provides no additional information about the sample. The adjective "representative" has no technical definition and simply represents a subjective judgment on the part of the term's user. No objective criteria are established to determine if a sample is or is not representative. Frequently, however, "representative sample" is the only description of the sample that is provided. Dropping the adjective and including a description of the sample selection process and information on the correspondence between the sample and the population is recommended. The importance of the description is introduced in the next section.

SAMPLING AND VALIDITY

Rarely can a researcher collect data on all the subjects of interest in a particular study. Samples provide a practical and efficient means to collect data. The sample serves as a model of the population. However, for a researcher to extend study findings to the population, the model must be an accurate representation of the population.

The ability of a researcher or user of a study to extend findings beyond sample individuals, time, and place is referred to as "external validity" (Campbell & Stanley, 1963; Cook & Campbell, 1979). Cook and Campbell pose the central question for external validity by asking, "Given that there is probably a causal relationship from construct A to construct B, how generalizable is this relationship across persons, settings, and times?" (1979, p. 39). For example, researchers find that using a computer-assisted instruction software package for reading in the third grade in an inner-city school improved the students' vocabulary and comprehension. Consumers of this study could reasonably ask how the instructional method would work in rural schools? How about with fourth graders? Are the gains a product of the novelty of using the computer in the classroom that would not occur when the novelty wears off?

The ability to generalize study findings is a function of the sample from which the data are actually obtained. Both sampling design and execution have an impact on generalizability. The practical sampling approach taken in this book emphasizes both design and execution, for both can affect the validity or total error of the research. Sample design includes choosing an appropriate selection technique, such as random digit dialing, and determining the number of cases needed for the study. Executing a design includes obtaining a comprehensive listing of the population for the study, obtaining the data reliably, and insuring that responses are actually received from a group whose composition accurately represents the population. Any plan or action that affects the composition of the group from whom data are actually collected has a bearing on the generalization of the results.

Therefore, practical sampling design must be integrated throughout research design and execution.

In addition to external validity, the sample design is directly affected by and directly affects two statistical validity considerations included in Cook and Campbell's discussion of validity (1979). Statistical conclusion validity is the ability to reach conclusions about relationships that appear in the sample data, that is, covariation. Statistical tests are generally used to examine whether the relationship that is observed is due to change. Or as Kraemer and Thiemann state, "A *statistical test* defines a rule that, when applied to the data, determines whether the null hypothesis can be rejected, i.e., whether the evidence is convincing beyond reasonable doubt" (1987, p. 23). Because these tests are sensitive to both the size of the relationship (effect size) and the size of the sample, the sample size can be critical to avoid "false conclusions about covariation" (Cook & Campbell, 1979, p. 37).

Small sample size may contribute to a conservative bias (Type II error) in the application of a statistical test. A Type II error occurs when a null hypothesis is not rejected although in fact it is false. In this situation, the program or intervention being tested is judged ineffective even though it does have an effect. However, the "reasonable doubt" criterion may be impossible to meet given the expected effect size and the actual sample size. The conservative bias occurs in instances where a small effect or covariation is true but the sample size is not sufficient for the effect to register above the statistical significance threshold. This phenomenon can be especially frustrating in evaluations of pilot programs where the number of participants and sample size are small. Effects resulting from the program that are small but meaningful can fall prey to the lack of statistical significance. Therefore, evaluators may wrongly conclude that the program failed to work effectively. This problem of sample size and statistical conclusion validity, referred to as power, is discussed in Chapter 7. (See Kraemer & Thiemann, 1987; Oakes, 1986; or Lipsey, 1989; for a more detailed explanation.)

A second aspect of statistical conclusion validity—reliability of measures—impacts sampling considerations. The less reliable an instrument is, the greater the observed variation in the data (Cook & Campbell, 1979). When observed variation increases, it becomes more difficult to reject the null hypothesis, even though a true relationship exists. To some extent, larger sample sizes can compensate for the increased variation, assuming the instrument is unbiased. However, to compensate for the inflation of the variance due to the lack of reliability of the instrument, it must be recognized and accounted for early in the design process.

WHY SAMPLE?

Given the mine field of validity concerns, a researcher is likely to ask, "Why sample?" Sampling is ultimately a practical means to an end. Researchers usually begin with a target population, often defined by a policy or program about which they ask a question. For example, a researcher could ask "Do developmental preschool programs for at-risk 4-year-olds improve cognitive gains and decrease the need for special-education assistance for these students in later years?" A target population of at-risk 4-year-olds as defined by policymakers is included in the research question.

The researcher transforms the research question into a feasible empirical project through the use of sampling. Clearly, it is not likely that all at-risk 4-year-olds can be provided with the development program and tested over a period of years to determine the impact of the program. Resource limitations prevent this. In this case, the limitations occur from both the programmatic and research concerns. Finding funds, facilities, and trained personnel to provide the developmental programs would be difficult. Equally difficult would be the investment in data collection, analysis, and follow-up needed for the evaluation. Nor would it be prudent to expend public funds for the program without an evaluation of its impact.

Sampling allows the use of a subset of the target population for testing the program. The principal reason for sampling is the resource constraint on the research project. But sampling can also *improve quality*. For example, limitations on the number of trained individuals that can competently administer pretests on 3- and 4-year-olds may necessitate hiring untrained staff or utilizing tests for at-risk status that are too simplistic to produce reliable results. Sampling can allow resources to be directed to improve the amount and quality of data on each individual and minimize problems of missing data.

Researchers can encounter situations where sampling is not advisable. Two situations come to mind: sampling from small populations and sampling that may reduce credibility of results. When dealing with small populations (less than 50 members), collecting data on the entire population often improves the reliability and credibility of the data. The influence of a single extreme case or outlier in the data is much more pronounced with small samples, and testing hypotheses becomes much simpler with population data. Also, if study consumers know that a "unique case" was omitted from the sample, the credibility of the results can be damaged. This type of problem is more likely to occur with a small population where consumers have more detailed information concerning individual members of the population.

The credibility of a study may also be adversely influenced by sampling in a study that may lead to recommendations about the distribution of public funds. For example, using a sample of political subdivisions—cities and counties—to test relationships between local characteristics and the need for funds may prove statistically efficient but politically intolerable. Again, the credibility of results in the users' minds—legislators in this case—may be reduced if their locality is not represented in the analysis. A researcher cannot state unequivocally that the results would not have been affected by the presence of the legislator's home locality in the study. The omission of a locality in this example may allow a wedge to be driven in, which would preclude use of the study.

Sampling for studies where the results are to be used in the political environment may require an additional layer of concern for political credibility beyond scientific concerns for validity. But this is not to say that sampling is not to be undertaken for policy studies.

In instances where sampling is not undertaken, some of the concerns addressed in the sample design remain relevant. For example, obtaining a comprehensive list of the target population is one of the first concerns for sampling. A census survey of all members of the target population also requires a comprehensive list. Research issues related to coverage of the target population and nonresponse (that is, cases for which data are missing) are relevant for studies that do not use samples as well as for those that do.

OVERVIEW OF THE BOOK

The "practical sampling design" approach used in this book extends beyond the boundaries of sampling theory. Practical sampling design includes sampling theory, logic of the design, and execution of the design. The logic of the sample design and its execution permeate the entire study approach. The nature of the study, measures and instruments, data collection method, study population definition, and the analysis of the data affect and are affected by the sample approach. Practical sampling design must be integrated into the study approach to improve the validity of the results.

The importance of integrating practical sampling design considerations and current recognition of the extent of the sampling considerations for the design is illustrated by a common situation that occurs when a sampling consultant begins to work with a research team. The team usually begins by asking "What size sample do we need to generalize the results to the population?'' The sampler responds by asking, ''What do you want to find out, about whom?'' Research teams sometimes restrict the role of sampling to the single question of sample size. To improve the validity and reduce total error, the implications of sampling must be included throughout the study.

This book presents an approach to sample design that provides a basis for making decisions about design alternatives throughout the research process. This approach is labeled *practical sample design*. The term ''practical'' is used because a framework that presents alternatives and guidance for choosing between the alternatives is emphasized, rather than sampling theory. The book is conceptual and provides detailed examples of selecting alternatives in actual sampling practice. It is not heavily theoretical or mathematical, although the material is based on the theoretical and mathematical sampling work that has preceded it and provides references for those interested in proceeding deeper into the literature.

The book is oriented toward the researcher who needs to apply sampling as a research tool. As such, it is targeted for graduate methods courses in social and policy sciences that need a supplemental sampling test to help prepare researchers. Also, it could be a reference for sample design by researchers who need advice on sampling in planning their research. However, researchers who are planning large, complex samples would be well advised to seek the assistance of an experienced sampler.

Chapter 2 describes two sample selection approaches—nonprobability and probability sampling. Several basic designs illustrate each approach. Chapter 3 presents the practical sampling design approach. It contains two distinct parts: a presentation of the sources of total error in probability sampling and an outline of the framework for practical sample design. Taken together these two parts explain why sample design must be integrated into the overall research design and execution. Realistic alternatives, criteria for selecting among the alternatives, and implications for other choices are all part of the practial sampling design approach.

Chapter 4 presents four detailed examples from the research literature. The examples are described using the organization of the practical sample design framework, explained in Chapter 3. The examples illustrate a wide variety of studies with different types of populations, data collection methods, and sample designs.

The remaining three chapters draw on the examples for illustrations. Chapter 5 deals with sampling frames, Chapter 6 with sampling techniques, and Chapter 7 discusses sample size. The final chapter covers postsampling choices.

2

Sample Selection Approaches

Approaches to sample selection fall into two broad categories: probability and nonprobability sampling. Probability samples are selected in such a way that every member of the population actually has a possibility of being included in the sample. Nonprobability samples are selected based on the judgment of the researchers to achieve particular objectives of the research at hand. The primary focus of this book is on probability samples. The reason for this focus is that probability samples can be rigorously analyzed to determine possible bias and likely error. There is no such advantage for nonprobability samples. However, nonprobability samples are useful tools in certain circumstances.

NONPROBABILITY SAMPLING

Nonprobability samples are used for many research projects. These samples can be chosen for convenience or on the basis of systematically employed criteria. Nonprobability samples are actually a collection of sampling approaches that have the distinguishing characteristic that subjective judgments play a role in the selection of the sample. Subjective judgments are used to determine the units of the population that are contained in the sample. The selection method for nonprobability samples contrasts with that of probability samples that are selected by a randomized mechanism that assures selection independent of subjective judgments.

Six frequently used nonprobability sample designs are:

Conveniences samples
Most similar/most dissimilar samples
Typical case samples
Critical case samples
Snowball samples
Quota samples

The six nonprobability samples are summarized in Table 2.1.

TABLE 2.1
Nonprobability Sample Designs

Type of Sampling	Selection Strategy
Convenience	Select cases based on their availability for the study.
Most Similar/Dissimilar Cases	Select cases that are judged to represent similar conditions or, alternatively, very different conditions.
Typical Cases	Select cases that are known beforehand to be useful and not to be extreme.
Critical Cases	Select cases that are key or essential for overall acceptance or assessment.
Snowball	Group members identify additional members to be included in sample.
Quota	Interviewers select sample that yields the same proportions as the population proportions on easily identified variables.

Convenience sampling. A convenience sample is a group of individuals who are readily available to participate in a study. For instance, psychologists interested in the relationship between violence in movies and aggressive behaviors by the American public may use volunteers from an introductory psychology class in an experiment. Student volunteers respond to questions related to their attitudes about and propensity toward violence and are observed playing games with contrived conflict situations. Then the students are split into two groups that have been determined by *random assignment*. Random assignment refers to a technique that assigns the student volunteers to a treatment group and a control group. It differs from random sampling. Random sampling refers to a probability method of selecting the entire sample, that is, the members of both groups. Convenience sampling is used in this example, not random sampling. When the sample is later divided into two groups, in this case, random assignment is used.

One group is shown a movie with graphic violence; the other group is shown a movie without violence. Both groups are subsequently interviewed, observed playing the games with potential conflict situations, and the differences in the attitudes and behaviors for the two groups before and after the movie are compared.

The students participating in this experiment are a convenience sample. They were part of an existing group from which it was easy for the researchers to obtain volunteers. Convenience of obtaining data met one of the researchers' objectives, but what knowledge has been gained about the impact of violent movies on the American public?

Conditions other than exposure to a violent movie may be theorized to increase the propensity toward violence. These other conditions are confounding variables, which make it difficult to ascertain the impact of the independent variable, in this case violent movies. For example, individual levels of stress may be hypothesized to relate to violent tendencies. Also, young people may be less inhibited and, therefore, more prone to violence.

To the extent that all the students in the sample (both the treatment and the control groups) had more or less stress than the adult population of the United States, their responses may not generalize to that population. Stress could also have been a confounding variable in differences between the treatment and control groups in terms of aggressive behavior. If the students had less stress than the population, finding that violent movies do not increase violent tendencies may not be valid for the adult population. The principal problem with the design is that the accuracy of using the sample as a model of the population with respect to the stress level, or any other hypothesized cause of violent behavior, is unknown. Therefore, it is not clear that the effect of the movie (or its lack) is applicable beyond the sample.

Age is a more observable source of confounding in this situation. College students are predominantly between the ages of 18 and 25. If younger adults are more prone to exhibit aggressive behavior, the sample would be likely to have results biased toward more aggressive responses. The choice of a convenience sample, in this illustration, is likely to have biased the results in such a way as not to allow their generalization to the population. Of course, other factors may also have an effect on violent attitudes and behaviors, and these factors may be unevenly distributed between the sample and the population.

The uncertainty and bias can be controlled in two ways; one uses more data to improve the convenience sample approach; the other requires abandoning the the convenience approach in favor of a probability sample. First, for characteristics that can be readily measured, such as age, explicit controls can be used. An alternative convenience sample with proportional representation from each age group could have been selected (but probably not from the psychology class).

For stress, it is more difficult to acquire information on stress levels in the population. This information would be necessary to group and select individuals proportionally. Random selection, which guarantees every member of the population a possibility of being selected, provides a measure of control over stress levels. Random selection is an implicit control used to obtain a mix of characteristics, including stress levels and other characteristics not explicitly controlled. Random selection, a characteristic of probability sampling, is explained in the next section.

It is worthwhile to note that the random assignment of the students to the treatment and control groups in this example addresses the selection bias associated with internal validity (Cook & Campbell, 1979). That is, differences between the treatment and control groups, both of which consist of volunteers from the college psychology class, in terms of the aggressive behaviors can be attributed to exposure to a violent movie. Random assignment has as its goal removing other variables that may account for the differences in the volunteers. However, random assignment does not affect the uncertainty and bias that would occur in extrapolating the effect found from the sample of volunteers to the American public. Generalizations are restricted by the use of a convenience sample in this illustration.

The literature on homeless populations and deinstitutionalization provides a concrete example of the use of convenience samples. As policymakers became more aware of the problem, the rush to provide empirical information concerning the homeless meant that much of the data were obtained through the use of convenience samples (Burnam & Koegel, 1988). Usually missions or other providers of beds for the homeless formed the locus from which respondents were selected and data were collected. The potential for bias existed because the rules governing who were eligible for beds excluded some individuals from the samples. Furthermore, some homeless were not willing to or capable of going through the procedures required to obtain a bed.

Recently, two studies of the homeless population have attempted to provide information based on probability sampling approaches. These approaches, described in Rossi, Wright, Fisher, and Willis (1987) and Burnam and Koegel (1988), require more time and a larger budget than the convenience approaches. But they are pointing to some substantial differences. For example, Burnam and Koegel report that less than half (44.2%) of the homeless slept in a mission or shelter bed, in contrast to an earlier estimate of nearly two thirds (66%), based on a convenience sample.

Most similar/dissimilar case sampling. Most similar and most dissimilar samples are varieties of purposeful samples that are often used in comparative government research and case study approaches to policy studies. Western nations, such as the United States, Canada, England, France, Germany, and Italy, are often grouped and used as a sample of countries for comparing relationships between political, social, and economic systems. Other groupings, for example developing nations, are often chosen for studies such as the impact of increasing national debt on the standards of living in the countries. Case studies often select the "best" and "worst" cases to contrast policy implementation in most dissimilar designs.

These studies are useful given the limited number of cases, limited resources, and the need for comparative information, but questions arise concerning the ability of the findings to be extended beyond the actual cases studied. Often, a locality will compare itself with surrounding localities when considering property tax rates or judging the adequacy of state funds. Geographic proximity is the operational definition of similarity in this case. These comparisons may or may not accurately show the locality's relative position with respect to localities that are similar in terms of tax base or ability to raise local revenues.

Typical case sampling. Nonprobability samples are often selected when extreme limitations on time and resources prohibit probability samples. "Typical case" designs exemplify designs developed under these circumstances. For this design, the researchers select a few cases that are felt to be normal or usual. To increase the credibility of the design, cases that are considered unique or special are not included in the sample.

However, the researchers' judgment and knowledge of the population is crucial for this design to be credible. In policy research, "typical case" samples often engender very close scrutiny. Suspicion of bias in the selection is a common problem. Using "typical cases" invites close inspection of the cases selected, and often the credibility of the findings is tarnished when a case appears atypical. The method of selecting cases for this type of design focuses attention on each individual case. The sample becomes the focus of scrutiny.

Critical case sampling. Another nonprobability sample design that is similar in many ways to "typical case" design is the "critical case" design. For critical case designs, the researcher selects a limited number of cases that logic or prior experience indicate will allow generalization to the population. Selection of key precincts to predict election results can be based on critical case logic. An extreme application of this design is signaled in the statement, "As Maine goes, so goes the nation." Using Maine as the critical case held up well until the 1948 presidential election when a majority of voters in Maine cast ballots for Dewey. A wag then coined the slogan "As Maine goes, so goes Vermont."

Snowball sampling. A distinct variety of nonprobability samples is the snowball sample. Snowball sampling relies on previously identified group members to identify other members of the population. As newly identified members name other members, the sample grows like a snowball. Often snowball sampling is used when a population listing is unavailable and cannot be compiled by researchers. Sociological research on groups as diverse as illegal drug users, illegal aliens, and community "power elites" uses this method of generating a sample of the population.

Quota sampling. Another variety of nonprobability sampling is the quota sample. Quota sampling divides the population group being studied into subgroups, for instance male and female or black, white, Hispanic, American Indian, and other ethnic groups. Then, based on proportions of the subgroups needed for the final sample, interviewers are given a number of units from each subgroup that they are to select and interview. The quota sample has many similarities with probability samples, in particular with stratified probability samples, but it differs in one important respect. Quota sampling allows interviewer discretion in the selection of the individuals for the sample. Interviewers are provided with explicit instructions about the characteristics of the individuals that they are expected to interview. For example, the number of respondents from a specific neighborhood and the number of blacks and whites, or males and females may be specified in the assigned quotas. Usually the numbers are established to make the overall sample proportions identical to population proportions.

However, the interviewer selects the interviewee. Stuart (1984) points out the three major problems that this aspect of quota sampling causes:

> As will be evident from this interviewer freedom, the danger of selection bias is always present in quota sampling; and of course, since the procedure for selecting the sample is ill-defined, there is no valid method of estimating the standard error of a sample estimate . . . quota sampling conceals the[se] problems of *nonresponse.* (p. 43, emphasis in original)

The problem of nonresponse is concealed in quota sampling because the interviewer, when faced with a refusal or a household where no one is found at home, simply selects another household. Thus, the interviewer always obtains the required number of interviews but may underrepresent the portion of the population that is difficult to reach.

Cook and Campbell propose a particular variety of quota sampling, which they refer to as "the model of deliberate sampling for heterogeneity" (1979). The strategy of quota sampling they offer includes obtaining sample members from a wide range of backgrounds and conditions that are expected to influence the results: "Thus, a general education experiment might be designed to include boys and girls from cities, towns, and rural settings who differ widely in aptitude and in the value placed on achievement in their home settings" (p. 75). However, the design's shortcoming is in the ability to generalize from it. The most that researchers can say is that "we learned that the effect (or lack of effect) holds with at least one sample" (Cook & Campbell, 1979, p. 76). While this level of statement is accurate, confounding variables may void the finding with a different sample. Without knowing preexisting conditions of the sample, the utility of the sample for theory building is limited. Further, limiting findings to a particular sample is not adequate for providing information to influence policy.

Quota samples have, for the reasons given above, fallen out of favor as a sampling method. This has occurred in spite of the fact that quota samples are usually less expensive than probability samples. An approach, which has some characteristics of the quota sample but is actually a probability sample with quotas, is sometimes used for household-based studies. The probability sample with a quota uses specific geographic locations and a travel pattern for the interviewer to follow to obtain interviews along with the quotas.

Sudman (1976) describes the basis for this type of sampling being considered a probability sample:

> In probability sampling with quotas, the basic assumption is that it is possible to divide the respondents into strata in which the probability of being available for interviewing is known . . . Any respondent's probability of being interviewed is the product of his initial selection probability times his probability of being available for interviewing. (p. 193)

However, probability sampling with quotas is a biased sampling technique, although the bias is generally small. In addition, sampling error is higher than for other probability samples of similar size (Hess, 1985).

UTILITY OF NONPROBABILITY SAMPLES

Nonprobability sampling is a useful and expedient method of selecting a sample in certain circumstances. In many situations it is appropriate, and in some cases it is the only method available. For instance, in studies of certain special populations, such as illegal drug users, it would be impossible to put together a list needed to draw a probability sample. The referral method used in snowball sampling may be the only viable approach.

On occasions when the researcher is truly interested in particular members of the population that comprise the sample, rather than the population, a nonprobability sample may be more appropriate. For example, some comparative government studies are more interested in specific countries than in groups of countries (e.g., developing debtor nations).

In exploratory research situations where the researcher is attempting to determine whether a problem exists or not, a nonprobability statement may be a practical choice. A small pilot study with cases that would be likely to exhibit the problem could be conducted. The data could be used to examine whether a problem exists or not. This approach would not allow the estimation of the extent of the problem, but it may be an efficient use of scarce resources prior to determining whether a systematic study should be undertaken.

While the necessity of a nonprobability sample may be apparent in many cases, its use increases the uncertainty in using the sample data to represent the population. Kalton (1983) concisely summarizes the source of concern:

> Nonprobability sampling covers a variety of procedures, including the use of volunteers and the purposive choice of elements for the sample on the grounds that they are "representative" of the population. The weakness of all nonprobability sampling is its subjectivity, which precludes the development of a theoretical framework for it. (p. 7)

Because of the subjective nature of the selection process, nonprobability samples add uncertainty when the sample is used to represent the population as a whole. Confounding variables can influence the study results. The accuracy and precision of statements about the population can only be determined by subjective judgment. The selection procedure does not provide rules or methods for inferring sample results to the population, in contrast to probability sampling, as is pointed out later. Therefore, there is a risk that the findings are not valid because of bias in the selection process.

While the greatest risk in using purposeful samples is the problem with external validity, the credibility of the findings is also at risk. The question often arises, "what would the selection of other units for the sample show?" Bias, often unintended, in the selection process can produce results that are different from those expected for the population. An unbiased selection process is the only method that guarantees an unbiased sample.

Stuart (1984) states that "The sample itself can never tell us whether the process that engendered it was free from bias. We must know what the process of selection was if we are not forever to be dogged by the shadow of selection bias" (p. 4). Thus, credibility of the purposeful sample results relies on each individual's assessment of the selection and sample units. Even with the conformance to population proportions produced with quota sampling, the selection is biased in favor of interviewing individuals in the population that are easier to reach and interview. The bias in this case is masked by the proportions.

In sum, nonprobability sampling is the only recourse for obtaining data in certain situations. Limited resources, inability to identify members of the population, and need to establish the existence of a problem could justify the use of a nonprobability sample. However, the researcher should be well aware of the risks posed by using a nonprobability sample—risks to the validity and credibility of the study findings. Probability samples, discussed in the next section of this chapter, should be carefully considered and alternative techniques for conducting a probability sample fully examined before using a nonprobability sample.

Perhaps the most famous example of error in nonprobability sampling came in the presidential election of 1948. Three prominent polling firms, using quota samples, were convinced that Thomas Dewey would defeat Harry Truman by a significant margin. Truman actually received 50% of the popular vote, compared with Dewey's 45%. The subjective bias of the interviewers toward selecting Republicans for interviews resulted in the error in the prediction, even though the sample proportions matched the voting population proportions in terms of location, age, race, and economic status. The unintentional bias on the accuracy and credibility of polls caused polling firms to begin to use more costly probability samples.

PROBABILITY SAMPLING

Probability samples have the distinguishing characteristic that each unit in the population has a known, nonzero probability of being included in the sample. The probability of selection is not always the same for all members of the population, however. Sampling designs that give every member of the population the same probability of selection are referred to as equal probability samples. Unequal probability of selection samples occur when some members of the population are more likely to appear in the sample than others. Researchers must adjust unequal probability sample data to compensate for the differences in the likelihood of some population members appearing in the sample. The adjustments are accomplished by giving some cases greater influence or weight in the estimations. For example, if some members of the population are four times as likely to be selected as other members, their weight in the estimates must be reduced by one quarter, or a weight of .25. Reducing the influence of these cases will control for the fact that four times as many of these members are likely to appear in the sample. Weights, based on the probability of selection, allow unbiased representation of the population from an unequal probability sample.

Some units in a probability sample can be selected with certainty, a probability of one. These are units that the researcher judges to be absolutely required for the sample. For example, any survey of Illinois localities would normally include Chicago-Cook County with certainty. Chicago-Cook County would represent itself in the sample, and adjustments to the estimates made using the sample would be required to compensate for the differences in the probability of selection.

Probability samples imply the use of a random selection mechanism. Random selection eliminates subjective bias in the selection process and underlies the theories used to infer the sample results to the population. Random selection mechanisms include either using a lottery procedure with well-mixed numbers, extracting a set of numbers from a listing of random numbers, or using a computer program to generate a random list of units from an automated listing.

Random does not mean arbitrary or haphazard. Random selection is a very careful, specific procedure that insures that the selection of each unit in the sample is independent of the selection of any other unit. Randomness translates to the independence of each selection, that is, the selection of any population member does not affect the likelihood of any other population member being selected. Truly random processes are difficult to achieve and are often subject to human errors. McKean (1987), in an article titled "The Orderly Pursuit of Pure Disorder," shows the sensitivity of a process that is generally regarded as random in the example of the draft lottery of 1969:

> Capsules containing all the January birth dates were put in a box and mixed up; then all the February dates; then all the March dates, and so forth. As a result, dates that fell late in the year didn't get as thoroughly stirred up as those from early in the year. And the night the capsules were drawn, birthdays late in the year turned up first: a December date had a better than even chance of being among the first third selected. The next year draft officials mixed the dates better, and the problem was solved. (p. 75)

Five basic techniques for selecting probability samples are:

Simple random sampling
Systematic sampling
Stratified sampling
Cluster sampling
Multistage sampling

A brief definition of each type of sample is given below. Table 2.2 provides a summary for reference. Chapter 6 provides requirements, advantages, and disadvantages of each sampling technique.

TABLE 2.2

Probability Sample Designs

Type of Sampling	Selection Strategy
Simple Random	Each member of the study population has an equal probability of being selected.
Systematic	Each member of the study population is either assembled or listed, a random start is designated, then members of the population are selected at equal intervals.
Stratified	Each member of the study population is assigned to a group or stratum, then a simple random sample is selected from each stratum.
Cluster	Each member of the study population is assigned to a group or cluster, then clusters are selected at random and all members of a selected cluster are included in the sample.
Multistage	Clusters are selected as in the cluster sample, then sample members are selected from the cluster members by simple random sampling. Clustering may be done at more than one stage.

Simple random sampling. Simple random samples are selected such that each member of the study population has an equal probability of selection. All members of the study population are either physically present or listed, and the members are selected at random until a previously specified number of members or units has been selected.

Using the convention that 'n' represents the number of units in the sample and 'N' the number of units in the study population, simple random samples have the property that every subset of n units is equally likely to be selected from the N units of the population. The probability of selection for each member of the study population is

$$p = f = n/N$$

where p is the probability of selection, and
f is the sampling fraction.

For example, in a study of the advanced elderly, 1,600 adults over 75 are selected from the 625,000 members of that population. The probability of an individual's selection is 1,600/625,000 or .0026.

Simple random selection in this text will be assumed to be selection without replacement. This means that once a unit is selected in the sampling process, it is removed from the pool eligible for future selection. This contrasts with selection with replacement where the selected unit is returned to the pool eligible for selection. While the latter has desirable statistical properties, it has the potential undesirable practical consequence of selecting a particular unit multiple times.

Systematic sampling. Systematic samples are sometimes referred to as "pseudo-simple random samples" because they have properties similar to simple random samples, but this method of selection is easier to apply in certain field situations. A systematic sample is selected by first assembling the population or a listing of the population, choosing a random start, and then selecting every ith unit (e.g., 6th or 234th). The random start is an essential component of the process. Without using random start, some members of the study population have a zero probability of selection, and the sample cannot be considered a probability sample.

The selection interval, i, is determined by the formula

$$i = N/n = 1/f$$

Simplicity of field operations dictate that the interval must be an integer. A recommended procedure when the division produces a fraction is to round down to the next integer, that is, 12.895 would be rounded down to 12. Because of the rounding down, more than n units would be selected. Then the units in excess of the n required would be removed through a second random selection procedure. For example, if a sample of 1,000 is desired, rounding the selection interval from 12.895 to 12 would be expected to yield approximately 1,075 cases in the sample. Seventy-five cases can be selected, using a simple random sampling procedure, and eliminated from the sample before data are collected.

A problem can occur with systematic sampling if the population listing is arranged in cyclical fashion and the cycle coincides with the selection interval. If the interval 12 is chosen and the data are listed by month, the data from the same month would be selected for each year. Cyclical listings of the population are to be avoided, or units should be rearranged when using systematic sampling.

Stratified sampling. Stratified sampling requires that the members of the survey population be divided into groups, called strata, before the sampling process begins. Each unit is assigned to one and only one stratum based on prior knowledge about the unit. Then, independent random samples are selected from each stratum using a procedure analogous to one of the two described for simple random sampling or systematic sampling.

Stratified sampling can be carried out in such a manner that the same sampling fraction, f, is used in each stratum. Known as proportionate stratified sampling, this is an equal probability of selection method. Alternatively, sampling fractions can be set at different rates for each stratum. Using different sampling fractions leads to unequal probability of selection and is called disproportionate stratified sampling. Disproportionate stratified sampling requires additional work on the part of the researcher (e.g., weighting the responses for analysis), but payoffs in increased precision can justify the additional work.

Proportionate stratification is often done to insure representation of groups that have importance to the research or for the policy decisions. For example, in a statewide study of advanced elderly, it may be considered important to represent each region of the state. Disproportionate stratification usually is done to allow analysis of some particular strata members or to increase the overall precision of the sample estimates. Strategies and implications of disproportionate stratification are explained in Chapter 6.

Cluster sampling. Cluster sampling has a superficial similarity with stratified sampling in that survey population members are divided into unique, nonoverlapping groups prior to sampling. The groups are referred to as clusters in this case. Clusters are often naturally occurring groupings such as schools, households, or geographic units such as city blocks. The clusters are then randomly selected and each member of the cluster is included in the sample. The cluster is the sampling unit in this case, not the individual member of the population.

Contrasting cluster sampling with stratified sampling, a cluster sample involves the selection of a few groups and data are collected from all group members, while stratified sampling involves selecting a few members from each group or stratum. A school example is relevant. To sample students from a school, each student could be placed in a stratum by grade, then a few students from each grade could be randomly selected for a stratified sample. Alternatively, students could be divided into clusters by classrooms. Then, a sample of classrooms would be chosen, and all students in the selected classrooms would be used as the sample.

Selecting the clusters randomly meets the criteria imposed to make cluster sampling a probability sampling technique. Table 2.3 shows the calculation of the probability of selection for a cluster sample. The example is based on a population of 5,000,000 (N) household units that are grouped into 100,000 clusters (C). Forty clusters (c) are chosen at random in this example. Clusters in this example could be based on census tracts in a city. Since the average cluster size is approximately 50 and all households in the selected clusters are included, the sample size (n) will be 2,000 (50 × 40). The overall probability of selection is .0004 (2,000/5,000,000 = .0004), even though the clusters have different numbers of households.

TABLE 2.3
Probability of Selection for Cluster Sampling

Population Information
  Number of population members: $N = 5,000,000$
  Number of clusters in the population: $C = 100,000$
  Average cluster size $= 50$

Sample Information
  Sample size: $n = 2,000$
  Number of clusters in the sample: $c = 2,000/50 = 40$
  Probability: $p = 40/100,000 = (50)(40)/5,000,000 = .0004$

Whereas the use of stratification generally improves the precision of statistics, clusters usually have the opposite effect. Clustering usually decreases the precision of the statistics. The use of cluster sampling is usually justified on practical grounds. Cluster samples can be obtained without having lists of the entire population and allow a substantial reduction in transportation and training costs when personal interviews are to be used to collect data.

Multistage sampling. The concept underlying cluster sampling is used and extended in multistage sampling. The simplest type of multistage sampling is two-stage sampling. In the first stage, groupings of the study population members, known as primary sampling units (PSUs), which are analogous to clusters, are selected. In the second stage, members of the population are randomly selected from the previously selected primary sampling units.

The probability of selection is determined by the cumulative probability of selection. Thus, unequal probabilities in one stage can be compensated for in the succeeding stage to produce an equal probability of selection overall. Table 2.4 illustrates two possible situations. In Table 2.4a, 500 PSUs are selected with equal probabilities, then 4 households are selected from each PSU. Unequal probabilities of selection result because the primary sampling units contain different numbers of members. In the table, examples of PSUs with 50 units and 100 units are shown. The cases selected from the primary sampling units with 50 units have a probability of selection of .0004. Cases selected from a primary sampling unit that is twice as large, 100 units, have one-half the probability of selection, .0002. The final example in Table 2.4b presents a probability proportionate to size (PPS) selection. PSUs are selected based on their relative size:

$$c \times N_c/N = p$$

TABLE 2.4

Probability of Selection for Multistage Samples

Number of population members: $N = 5,000,000$
Number of primary sampling units: PSU $= 100,000$
Sample size: $n = 2,000$

	Unequal Probability of Selection Sample		
a	*Stage 1*	*Stage 2*	*Probability of Selection*
Number of units in PSU	Select 500 PSUs with equal probability	× Select 4 units per PSU	
50	500/100,000	× 4/50 =	.0004
100	500/100,000	× 4/100 =	.0002

	Equal Probability of Selection Sample: Probability Proportionate to Size		
b	*Stage 1*	*Stage 2*	*Probability of Selection*
Number of units in PSU	Select 100 PSUs based on probability proportionate to size (PPS)	× Select 20 units per PSU	
50	100 (50)/5,000,000	× 20/50 =	.0004
100	100 (100)/5,000,000	× 20/100 =	.0004

where c is the number of PSUs selected,
N_c is the number of elements in a particular PSU,
N is the total number of elements, and
p is the probability of selection.

In the example, the probability of selecting the PSU that contains 50 cases is $100 \times 50/5,000,000$ or .001. The primary sampling unit with 100 cases is twice as likely to be selected ($p = .002$). However, by selecting an equal number of cases from all primary sampling units—20 in this case—the probability of selection for all final sampling units is equal ($p = .0004$). As a check, the overall probability of selection multiplied by the population should yield the sample size ($.0004 \times 5,000,000 = 2,000$).

The multistage approach requires trade-offs between improved precision of the sample estimates, lower costs of data collection, and greater complexity. As the number of stages increases, generally the precision decreases. Stratification can be added at any or all stages, which generally improves precision, but adds cost and complexity. A total of five stages is utilized in the National Household Survey conducted by the Survey Research Center at the University of Michigan. The stages and the stratifications are described in Chapter 4.

CONCLUSION

Sampling approaches fall into two categories, probability and nonprobability. Choosing between these two types of approaches is a matter of weighing the requirements for validity and credibility against a realistic assessment of the requirements for timeliness and effort of the alternative approaches. Probability sampling, carefully designed and carried out, has greater validity and credibility than nonprobability sampling. Often, although not always, the costs and time required to conduct a probability sample are greater than for a nonprobability sample.

The remainder of this book will deal exclusively with probability sampling. While nonprobability samples are useful in some situations, an underlying premise of this book is that probability samples are clearly the preferred alternative, and only in cases where probability samples cannot be used are nonprobability samples viable.

The next chapter brings the rationale behind this premise clearly into focus. The bias and likely error stemming from the use of a probability sample can be rigorously examined and estimated. No comparable examination and estimation can be conducted for nonprobability samples. Thus, the range of uncertainty stemming from the use of a sample can be estimated with a specified degree of confidence for probability samples, but not for nonprobability samples. Sampling theory, well developed and tested for probability sampling, accounts for this difference.

Chapter 3 and, in more detail, the subsequent chapters provide the researcher with the practical sample design approach, a framework to be used in designing and executing probability sampling. The framework and examples should be useful in helping the researcher develop a practical design given the study goals and the resources available. Understanding these tools is especially important to produce a sample with the best possible fit for the study.

3

Practical Sample Design

Practical sample design seeks to produce valid and credible sample data and statistics that match the precision needed for the study. Practical sample design is an approach that integrates sampling design and execution into the overall research process using the concept of total error for the assessment of validity, credibility, and precision. The validity of the data affects the accuracy of inferring sample results to the population and drawing correct conclusions from the tests of hypotheses. Credibility, in large measure, rests on the sample selection process. Using random selection removes subjective judgment from the selection of the sample and enhances credibility.

The concern for precision arises as an intrinsic consequence of sampling. Selecting a subset of the population means that some members of the population are not included in a sample. Repeated selection of samples using the same procedure will yield different results because of this. Fortunately, sampling theory provides us with much useful information about the fluctuation of sample results. Using sampling theory, the probable amount of fluctuation or sampling variability can be calculated. The relationship between sampling variability and precision is well established: precision of a sample statistic decreases as sampling variability increases. Sampling theory provides the researcher with knowledge of the factors that contribute to variability and, therefore, ways to reduce the variability to obtain an acceptable level of precision.

To begin to understand how choices should be made in the design process and to use the practical sample design approach, the sources of threats to validity and sampling variability must first be understood. The threats to external validity, described in Chapter 1, are usually known as bias in the sampling context. Bias in sample selection causes systematic differences between the sample and the population that the sample represents. Sources of bias mentioned in the previous chapter are differences between the target population and the study population and sampling methods that cause some subpopulations to be overrepresented in the sample.

Threats to statistical conclusion validity usually manifest themselves as increases in sampling variability. Increasing sampling variability does not cause systematic differences between the population and the sample, but it affects the precision of the estimates and may retard the ability to reach accurate conclusions. Bias and sampling variability together represent total error for the sample. Total error is systematically decomposed and analyzed in the next section. The final section of this chapter presents the practical sample design framework, which provides guidance for making sampling choices that reduce, to the extent possible, bias and sampling variability.

SOURCES OF ERROR IN SAMPLING DESIGN

The goal of practical sampling design can be achieved by minimizing the amount of total error in the sample selection to an acceptable level given the purpose and resources available for the research. Total error has three distinct components:

Nonsampling bias: systematic error due to differences in population definition or measurement error, for example.

Sampling bias: systematic error that results from a sampling approach that over-represents a portion of the study population.

Sampling variability: the fluctuation of sample estimates around the study population parameters that results from the random selection process.

Each component generates concerns for the researcher. However, only the final two components are generally considered in the domain of the sampling design. Frequently, discussions of error in samples dwell exclusively on sampling variability and its estimate, the standard error or sampling error. All three sources of error should be explicitly considered for effective sampling designs.

Total error is defined as the difference between the true population value for the target population and the estimate based on the sample data. Total error for the mean is:

$$E = X_T - \bar{x}$$

where X_T is the true population value, and
$\bar{x}$ is the sample mean.

Because total error affects the extent to which the study objectives are met, practical sample design must take all three components into account. Each of the three components of total error, the point in the research process they can arise, and some examples of the sources of each are graphically illustrated in Figure 3.1. Furthermore, sample design takes place under

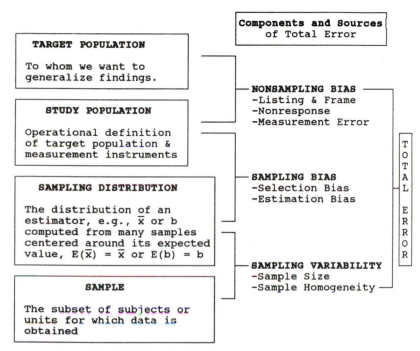

Figure 3.1. Practical Sampling Design

resource constraints. Decisions that allocate resources to reduce error from one component necessarily affect the resources available for reducing error from the other two components. Trade-offs are essential in practical sampling design. Limited resources, which are the case in practical design situations, force the researcher into making trade-offs between reducing the components of total error. The researcher must be fully aware of the three components of error to make decisions based on the trade-offs to be considered in reducing total error.

Nonsampling bias. Nonsampling bias is the difference between the true target population value and the population value obtained if the data collection operations were carried out on the entire population. Nonsampling bias results from explicit decisions and implementation of decisions during data collection efforts that are not directly related to the selection of the sample. For example, the definition of the study population may exclude some members of the target population that the researcher would like to include in the study findings. Even if data were collected on the entire *study* population in this case, the findings would be biased because of the exclusion of some *target* population members. The formula for nonsampling bias using the mean as an example of the population value is:

$$\text{NSB} = \bar{X}_T - \bar{X}_S$$

where $\bar{X}_T$ is the true mean of the target population, and
$\bar{X}_S$ is the mean obtained from the study population.

Differences in the true mean of the population and the survey population mean arise from several sources. The principal difference relevant to sample design is the difference between the target population and the study population. The target population is the group about which the researcher would like to make statements. The target population can be defined based on conditions and concerns that arise from the theory being tested or by concerns generated from the policy being examined. For instance, in a comprehensive needs assessment for the homeless, the target population should include all homeless, whether served by current programs or not. On the other hand, an evaluation of the community mental health services provided to the homeless should include only homeless recipients of community mental health care. The target population for the needs assessment is more broadly defined and inclusive of all homeless, in contrast to the portion of that population that is the target population for the evaluation. The definition of the target population must be worked out from the study objectives.

The study population operationalizes the target population definition. Target populations are often dynamic, with new members being added and former members departing constantly. Target population listings can be incomplete and some members may not be identifiable. In other cases, study population members include individuals not within the target population. For example, researchers may be interested in the impact of development programs for 4-year-olds. The study population may include children from 3.5 to 5.5 years old in a pilot program conducted for the evaluation. The researchers would like to infer their research findings to 4-year-olds, even though the study population includes some children older than 4 and some younger. Since the age at which the developmental program is given may influence its impact, the expanded cohort may present a problem. However, problems with expanding the cohort in this case are lessened if the operational definition for the pilot program is the same definition that would be used if the program were implemented on a large scale. This issue should be brought up and discussed at the initiation of the program to insure that the pilot is consistent with the theory that underlies the implemented program and the intent of program sponsors.

In addition to definition problems that cause differences between the target and study population, nonresponse bias also creates differences. Nonresponse results from the inability to contact certain members of the population or the refusal of requests for data by some members. Absence from the class when cognitive tests were administered could cause nonresponse in the example of the developmental programs. If the nonresponse is truly random, it does not represent a bias. But this is frequently *not* the case. More frequently, the nonrespondents come from a definable subgroup of the population, and the omission of this subgroup from the data that are actually collected creates a bias in the results.

The researcher can never simply assume that nonresponse is unbiased. Usually nonresponses that result from research procedures (e.g., only contacting members of the population during the day rather than also attempting to contact them during the evening hours) or from refusals have a systematic pattern that leaves the nonrespondents underrepresented by the sample. The best way to deal with nonresponse bias is to reduce the existence of nonresponse, thereby reducing the proportion of the population that is underrepresented (Kalton, 1983, p. 64). Follow-ups to initial data collection attempts, trying multiple methods of contacting sample members, and using methods that minimize respondent refusals to participate are practical means of reducing nonresponse.

Other sources of nonsampling bias are measurement error and errors that occur in recording, coding, or transferring data. These two topics are beyond the scope of practical sampling design, although they are important considerations in reducing total error (see Raj, 1972). Implications of measurement error are discussed in Cook and Campbell (1979). Bradburn and Sudman (1980) provide insight from careful empirical research on reducing response bias in survey research through careful wording of items. Advice on reducing both sources of bias is provided in Fowler (1984) for survey research in general and in Lavrakas (1986) for telephone surveys in particular.

Sampling bias. Sampling bias is the difference between the study population value and the expected value for the sample:

$$SB = \bar{X}_S - E(\bar{x})$$

where SB is the sampling bias, and
$E(\bar{x})$ is the expected value of the mean.

The expected value of the mean is the average of the means obtained by repeating the sampling procedures on the study population. The expected value of the mean is equal to the study population value if the sampling and calculation procedures are unbiased.

Sampling bias can be subdivided into two components: (1) selection bias and (2) estimation bias. Selection bias occurs when not all members of the study population have an equal probability of selection. Estimation procedures can adjust for the unequal probabilities. The adjustments are made by using weights to compensate for the unequal probabilities of selection.

Selecting a sample from a study population list that contains duplicate entries for some members of the population provides an illustrative example of a selection bias. In the citizen survey example presented in Chapter 4, two lists are combined to form the study population list: state income tax returns and medicaid-eligible clients. An individual appearing on both lists would have twice the likelihood of being selected for the sample. It is impossible from a practical standpoint to purge the combined list of any duplicate listings. However, it is possible to adjust for the unequal probability of selection that arises.

To adjust for this unequal probability of selection, a weight (w) equal to the inverse of the increase in the probability of selection should be applied in the estimation process:

$$w = 1/p = 1/2 = .5$$

The probability of selection for this individual was twice the probability of selection for the study population appearing on the list only once. Therefore, this type of individual would receive only one-half of the weight of the other population members to compensate for their increased likelihood of appearing in the sample.

Estimation bias occurs when the average calculated using an estimation technique on all possible simple random samples from a population does not equal the study population value. For example, the median is a biased estimate of the population mean. Selection bias and estimation bias are intrinsically linked by using adjustments in the estimation to compensate for selection bias.

The concept of the expected value of the statistic undergirds sampling theory and provides the basis for many of the practical solutions used in modern sampling practice. The mean provides a convenient example to examine this concept in more detail, although any number of other estimators, such as the standard deviation or a regression coefficient, could be used. The expected value of the mean is the average of the means computed from repeated samples of the study population. Means computed from each sample form a distribution of values around the expected value of the mean. This distribution is known as the sampling distribution (Figure 3.2).

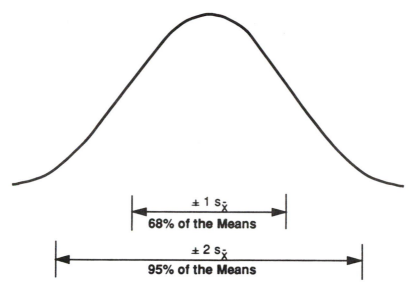

Figure 3.2. Sampling Distribution of the Mean

The sampling distribution when sample sizes reach 30 or more has the shape of the normal distribution, the familiar bell-shaped curve seen in Figure 3.2. This proves to be true no matter what the shape of the frequency distribution of the study population, as long as a large number of samples are selected.

Along with the mean (expected value), the standard deviation of the sampling distribution is another important attribute of the distribution. The properties of the normal distribution allow us to calculate the proportion of the sample means within a defined number of standard deviation units of the study population mean. Figure 3.2 illustrates the sampling distribution, its mean, and the percentage of the means within one or two standard deviation units of the average of the sample means.

Statistical theory also shows that the standard deviation of the sampling distribution ($s_{\bar{x}}$) is inversely related to the sample size. That is, the larger the sample size, the smaller the standard deviation of the sampling distribution. Figure 3.3 graphically shows this relationship.

Tables presenting the area under the normal curve can be used to calculate the percentage of sample means falling within specified standard deviation units. For smaller samples, the student t distribution can be used. For sample sizes below 30, values (the number of the standard deviation units) become larger for smaller sample sizes. For example, for a sample size

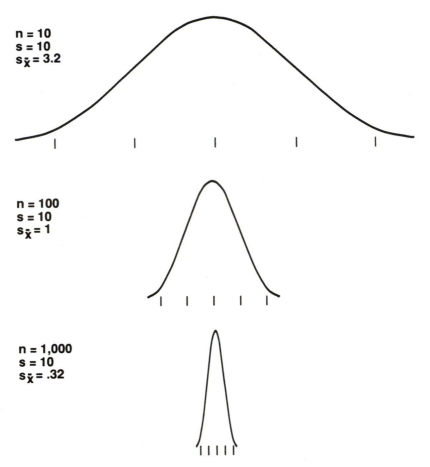

n = 10
s = 10
$s_{\bar{x}}$ = 3.2

n = 100
s = 10
$s_{\bar{x}}$ = 1

n = 1,000
s = 10
$s_{\bar{x}}$ = .32

Figure 3.3. Comparing Sampling Distributions with Alternate Sample Sizes

of 100, 95% of the sample means fall within ± 1.96 standard deviation units. A sample size of 10 (9 degrees of freedom) would require ± 2.26 standard deviation units to contain 95% of the sample means. As sample sizes decrease below approximately 30 units, the number of standard deviation units required to contain a specified proportion of sample means must increase. Thus, confidence intervals are larger for smaller samples. These t-values can be found in most tables showing the t distribution. First, compute the degrees of freedom (df) by subtracting one from the sample size ($n - 1$). In the case of a sample size of 10, the degrees of freedom would be 9. Then, select the column that indicates the level of one minus the probability level. That is for 95% probability, an $\alpha = .05$ is used. The column selected should be a two-tailed test. Make sure of this by referring to the directions associated with the table that you are using. If the table indicates a one-tailed test or only one side of the graphic is shaded, double the α. For example, for a table presenting one-tailed values, $\alpha = .025$ would be used for 95% confidence.

Finally, find the cell in the table at the intersection of the row with the appropriate degrees of freedom and the column with the selected probability level. For a sample size of 10, the t-value in the cell to be used for 95% confidence is 2.26, as shown below:

df	$\alpha = .05$	$\alpha = .01$
1	12.71	63.66
.	.	.
.	.	.
.	.	.
9	2.26	3.25
10	2.23	3.17

This means that 2.26 standard deviation units on each side of the mean will include 95% of the sample means. For a 99% confidence level, 3.25 standard deviation units are required.

Sampling variability. The final component of total error in a sample is directly attributable to the fact that statistics from randomly selected samples will vary from one sample to the next due to chance. In any particular sample, some members of the study population will be included and others will be excluded, producing this variation. For this reason, statistics are often noted to be random variables, varying by chance. Because statistics are not usually exactly equal to the study population value, it is useful to have an estimate of their proximity to the population value, in other words, their precision.

Using the properties of the sampling distribution, the interval in which 95% of the sample means fall can be computed:

$$E(\bar{x}) \pm 1.96(s_{\bar{x}})$$

where $s_{\bar{x}}$ is the standard deviation of the sampling distribution (standard error).

However, the practical problem a researcher is presented with is different than this. First, the researcher wishes to know how close the statistic calculated from sample data is to the population value. Second, the standard deviation of the sampling distribution is seldom known in actual research situations because only one sample rather than repeated samples are chosen.

The first problem is quickly overcome. The property, cited above, which indicates that a known percentage of the means in the sampling distribution fall within a related number of standard deviation units of the mean of the sampling distribution (e.g., 95% of the means fall within ± 2 $s_{\bar{x}}$) is used here. When the sample mean is calculated, an interval can be drawn around it such that the interval has a predetermined probability of containing the study population mean:

$$\bar{x} \pm t(s_{\bar{x}})$$

where t is the t-statistic for the predetermined probability level, and $s_{\bar{x}}$ is the standard error of the mean.

The interval drawn around the sample mean in this case is the interval within which the researcher expects that the true mean falls. The degree of confidence associated with this expectation is based on the predetermined probability of the selected t-statistic. The interval is often described as a confidence interval.

The second problem involves estimating the standard deviation of the sampling distribution or the standard error. Properties of the standard deviation of the population, its sample estimate, and the standard deviation of the sampling distribution must be used to solve this problem. The standard deviation of the population is the square root of the sum of squared deviations from the population mean divided by the number of units in the population:

$$S = (\Sigma(x_i - \bar{x})^2/N)^{\frac{1}{2}}$$

The population standard deviation can be estimated from the sample data using the following formula:

$$s = (\Sigma(x_i - \bar{x})^2/n - 1)^{\frac{1}{2}}$$

The standard deviation of the sampling distribution is the square root of the sum of the squared deviations of the sample means from the average of the sample means divided by the number of sample means:

$$S_{\bar{x}} = (\Sigma(\bar{x} - \bar{X})^2/m)^{\frac{1}{2}}$$

where m = the number of sample means.

This is referred to as the standard error or sampling error.

Sampling theory shows that the standard deviation of the sampling distribution is related to the sample estimate of standard deviation of the population by the following formula:

$$s_{\bar{x}} = s/(n)^{1/2}$$

From the formula, it can be deduced that two factors have an influence on sampling variability: the variability of the variable (standard deviation) and the size of the sample. Smaller standard deviations reduce the sampling error of the mean. The larger the sample, the smaller the standard deviation of the sampling distribution.

Since the standard deviation for the population can be estimated from the sample information and the sample size is known, a formula can be used to estimate the standard deviation of the sampling distribution, referred to hereafter as the standard error of the estimate, in this particular case, the standard error of the mean:

$$s_{\bar{x}} = s/(n)^{1/2}$$

$$s = (\Sigma(x_i - x)^2/n - 1)^{1/2}$$

where $s_{\bar{x}}$ is the estimate of the standard error,
$\quad\quad\quad s$ is the estimate of the standard deviation,
$\quad\quad\quad n$ is the sample size,
$\quad\quad\quad x_i$ are the sample observations, and
$\quad\quad\quad \bar{x}$ is the mean of the sample.

Using this formula allows the researcher to estimate the standard error, the statistic used to measure the final component of total error, based solely on information from the sample.

Probability sampling design discussions in this book assume that the sample would be selected without replacement; that is, once a unit has been randomly drawn from the population to appear in the sample, it is set aside and not eligible to be selected again. Sampling without replacement limits the cases available for selection as more are drawn from the population. The finite nature of the population under this condition may cause a finite population correction factor (FPC) to be needed in the computation of the standard error of the estimate.

For the standard error of the mean, the formula using the FPC is:

$$s_{\bar{x}} = (1 - n/N)^{1/2} s/(n)^{1/2}$$

As a rule of thumb, the sample must contain over 5% of the population to necessitate using the FPC. This is based on the fact that the finite population correction factor is so close to 1 when the sampling fraction is less than .05 that it does not appreciably affect the standard error calculation.

Standard error calculations are specific to the particular statistics being estimated. For example, the standard error for proportions is also commonly used:

$$s_p = ((pq)/n)^{1/2}$$

Most statistics textbooks present formulas for the standard error of several estimators. Also, they are calculated for the statistic being used by almost any statistical software package. These formulas, like the formulas presented above, assume that a simple random sample design has been used to select the sample. Formulas for more complex sampling techniques will be presented in Chapter 7.

One further note on terminology: sampling error and standard error are used interchangeably in the literature. They are specific statistics that measure the more general concept of sampling variability. Standard error, however, is the preferred term. The common use of the term sampling error is unfortunate for two reasons. First, it implies an error in procedures rather than a natural occurrence. Second, it often becomes substituted for the total error concept, which is more comprehensive. Examples of actual standard error calculations are shown in the examples in Chapter 4.

Total error. Sample design is a conscious process of making trade-offs to minimize the three components of total error. Too frequently, reducing the standard error becomes the exclusive focus of sample design because it can be estimated. Because the two bias components cannot be easily calculated, they are often given short shrift during the design process. However, failing sufficiently to consider and attempt to reduce all three components of total error can lessen the validity and credibility of the study findings.

The total error concept is summarized graphically in Figure 3.4. The top of the figure shows the frequency distribution of the target population, based on perfect information. The distribution includes a value for every member of the population arranged from low to high (left to right). Non-sampling bias is illustrated by the difference between the true mean of the target population and the observed mean of the study population. Non-sampling bias includes differences arising from the definition of the population, as well as errors attributable to instrumentation problems and field operations.

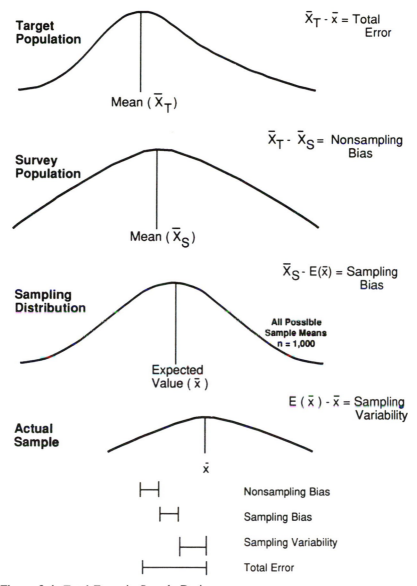

Figure 3.4. Total Error in Sample Design

Sampling bias is illustrated by the difference between the observed mean of the study population and the mean of the sampling distribution, $E(\bar{x})$. Differences here are due to bias in selection or bias in the estimation process. Finally, sampling variability is illustrated. It is the difference between the mean of the sampling distribution and its sample estimate, $\bar{x}$ in this case.

The next section presents the practical sample design framework that will assist the researcher in concentrating on total error and provide criteria for the decisions that are required in the design process.

PRACTICAL SAMPLING DESIGN FRAMEWORK

The framework for practical sampling design is a heuristic tool for researchers to use in sample design. The framework is, in essence, a series of choices that must be made, with each choice having implications for the integrity of the study. The purpose of providing the framework is to help researchers and consumers of research structure their thinking about design choices and the effects of their choices on total error.

The framework includes three phases of the overall design of the research project:

1. Presampling choices
2. Sampling choices
3. Postsampling choices

Presampling choices are the choices that researchers should make when the study is being designed. These choices set the stage for sampling choices, which follow and provide a base for analyzing total error. For example, one presampling choice is the definition of the target population. The definition of the target population relates to the study purpose. If the study is an evaluation of community mental-health services for the homeless, the target population could logically be defined as homeless who received any community mental health services in the state of Virginia between January 1987 and December 1988. This definition will be used as sampling choices concerning the listing of the target population from which the sample will be selected are made. Differences between the target population and the study population result in nonsampling bias.

Sampling choices are the usual fare for discussions of sampling. Each of these choices has direct and immediate impact on total error. One sampling choice is whether the probability of selection of the sample will be equal or unequal. If the probability is unequal and it is not adjusted through the use of weights, then sampling bias occurs.

Postsampling choices require decisions about procedures that are required after data are collected. One postsampling choice is the selection of a method to calculate standard errors. Usually, standard error calculations are based on sampling choices that have been made, particularly the type of sampling

TABLE 3.1

Questions for Sample Design

Presampling Choices
  1. What is the nature of the study—exploratory, descriptive, or analytical?
  2. What are the variables of greatest interest?
  3. What is the target population for the study?
  4. Are subpopulations or special groups important for the study?
  5. How will the data be collected?
  6. Is sampling appropriate?

Sampling Choices
  1. What listing of the target population can be used for the sampling frame?
  2. What is the tolerable error or estimated effect size?
  3. What type of sampling technique will be used?
  4. Will the probability of selection be equal or unequal?
  5. How many units will be selected for the sample?

Postsampling Choices
  1. How can nonresponse be evaluated?
  2. Is weighting necessary?
  3. What are the standard errors and related confidence intervals for the study estimates?

---

technique. Postsampling choices, such as this one, help to evaluate the extent of total error resulting from the sample, and, in other cases, reduce the total error.

This brief introduction to a few of the choices in the practical sampling framework demonstrates some interrelationships between choices made throughout the study process. The practical sampling design approach integrates sampling-related choices into research design and execution, rather than separating the sampling choices from the other study choices. A listing of the questions to be asked relevant to sampling choices appears in Table 3.1. Each of these questions is explained in the next sections of this chapter.

The practical sampling design choices represented by these questions bear directly on total error. Presampling choices relate primarily to nonsampling error. The choice concerning the need for analysis of subpopulations is one exception. If subpopulation analysis is a study objective, the sampling variability for the subpopulation analysis will be affected by the number of subpopulation members likely to be in the sample. A presampling choice to conduct subpopulation analysis can impact later sampling choices, such as the type of sampling technique. The sampling technique affects the number of subpopulation members in the sample and, therefore, the sampling variability for the subpopulation analysis.

Sampling choices have impact on all three components of total error. For example, the listing of the target population will affect the amount of nonsampling bias. A choice of unequal probability of selection will introduce bias into the sample. The number of units or subjects in the sample influences the sampling variability. Postsampling choices are ways of estimating, adjusting, or analyzing the components of total error.

PRESAMPLING CHOICES

What Is the Nature of the Study—Exploratory, Descriptive, or Analytical?

Exploratory research is generally conducted to provide an orientation or familiarization with the topic under study. It serves to enlighten the researcher about salient issues, helps focus future research on important variables, and generates hypotheses to be tested. Descriptive research is the core of many survey research projects where estimates of population characteristics, attributes, or attitudes are study objectives. Analytical research tests hypotheses, examining relationships between groups and/or relationships between variables. In practice, many studies attempt both descriptive and analytical tasks. It is important to understand this and establish priorities for the two tasks in these cases.

Exploratory research is often a preliminary activity leading to a more rigorous descriptive or analytical study. The sampling approach is usually severely limited by resource and time constraints. Small stratified probability samples or purposeful quota samples are frequently used to ensure that a wide range of groups are covered in the study. Broad coverage is more important in many exploratory research projects than reducing error since estimates, such as averages and proportions, are not reasonable study products.

Both descriptive and analytical studies are concerned with reducing total error. While they have similar objectives for reducing bias, the standard error component of total error is addressed differently. For descriptive studies, the focus is on the precision needed for the estimates. Needs assessments are one type of policy-related study where concern for precision of estimates is manifest. To make program decisions about the number of elderly that need services and the particular types of services needed, for instance, the samples are only useful if the estimates are sufficiently precise for budgetary and service delivery planning. For analytical studies, determining if the study will be powerful enough to reject the null hypothesis for the expected effect size is the relevant concern. This is done through a power test (Lipsey, 1989). Evaluation research, which often assesses the impact of a program on a target population, is likely to fall into the category of an analytical study.

What Are the Variables of Greatest Interest?

Selecting variables and estimating their variability is an important precursor to the sampling design. Studies often have multiple purposes. The researcher may envision many tables appearing in the write-up or using several statistical tools to test hypotheses. The selection of the variables of greatest interest will have important implications in the determination of sample size later on in the design process.

What Is the Target Population for the Study?

The target population for a study is the group for which the researchers would like to make general statements. The population can be individuals (residents of North Carolina or homeless in Los Angeles), groups of individuals (households in Richmond or schools in Wisconsin), or other elements (invoices, state-owned cars, or dwelling units). The theory being tested or the policy under study will help define the target population. Specific time frames, geographic location, age, and other relevant criteria are often used in the definition.

Are Subpopulations or Special Groups Important for the Study?

Often a researcher will choose to focus on a part of the target population for additional analysis of the phenomena being scrutinized. For example, households headed by single, working females were of particular interest to some scientists examining the impact of the income maintenance experiments (Skidmore, 1983). Design choices are available for instances when subgroups are known to be important for the study. A sample designed without taking the subpopulation into account can yield too few of the subpopulation members in the sample for reliable analysis. Increasing the overall sample size or disproportionately increasing the subgroup sample, if they can be identified before sampling, are potential remedies.

How Will the Data Be Collected?

Certain sampling choices can only be used in conjunction with certain data collection choices. For example, random digit dialing, a technique that generates a sample of randomly selected phone numbers, is an option when interviews are to be conducted over the phone. A probability sample of dwelling units is mainly useful for studies where on-site fieldwork, usually personal interviews, are to be used. Collecting data from administrative records or mailed questionnaires also poses specific sampling concerns. Mailed questionnaires typically have a high proportion of nonrespondents that affects the sampling variability and may cause nonsampling bias if the sample members that choose not to respond have similar characteristics.

In addition, the reliability of the responses achieved by the administration of the data collection instrument affects sampling considerations. Assuming that the instrument is unbiased, the central concern is that the less reliable an instrument is, the greater the standard error. Reliability of the instrument will be a consideration in selecting the sample size to avoid problems with statistical conclusion validity because of the inflation of the standard error.

Is Sampling Appropriate?

The decision to sample should be consciously made. Sampling is generally required to meet resource constraints. Furthermore, in many cases it will produce more accurate results than a population-census type study. Often, resources for studies of an entire population are consumed in attempting to contact all population members. Response to the first contact is often less than 50%, causing substantial nonsampling bias. Sampling the population would require fewer resources for the initial contacts and allow more resources to be invested in follow-up activities designed to increase response, paying dividends in lowering nonsampling bias. Also, having fewer cases by using sampling allows greater attention to accuracy in handling data. On the other hand, small populations and use of the information in the political environment may weigh against sampling. Careful consideration of the reasons for not sampling can be useful in designing a sample that will overcome most of the objections. For example, the political objection that every community in the state was not included when reviewing the program can be partially overcome if the sample can provide regional estimates.

SAMPLING CHOICES

What Listing of the Target Population Can Be Used for the Sampling Frame?

The sampling frame is the list from which the sample is selected. The sampling frame provides the definition of the study population and differences between the target population and sampling frame constitute a non-sampling bias. The sampling frame is the operational definition of the population, the group about which the researchers can reasonably speak. A telephone directory can provide the sampling frame for a study of the population in a community. It is an explicit sampling frame consisting of all households within the service area with working phones and listed numbers. For random digit dialing, the sampling frame is implicit, rather than explicit, that is, residences with working phones; no physical list of the population is obtained. Often, this frame is further refined by using a screen to determine if the residence has a member of the target population or to select a household member at random rather than selecting the individual that answers the phone by default.

Also, systematic, multistage, and cluster sampling do not necessarily require a physical listing of the entire target population. Systematic sampling is often done with the objects themselves, such as pulling invoices from a file cabinet or selecting individuals from a line in a soup kitchen. For cluster and multistage sampling, only a complete listing of the clusters or the sampling units is needed at each stage. Members of the target population are only listed in the final stage of multistage sampling and only for the sampling units selected in the stage immediately before.

Imperfect sampling frames can lead to nonsampling error. The most difficult imperfection to overcome is the omission of part of the target population from the sampling frame. This can lead to a bias that cannot be estimated for the sample data. Using multiple listings to formulate a frame, choosing a technique that does not require a frame, or conducting a special supplemental study to tap the omitted portion of the population are alternatives to ameliorate the problem or at least to estimate its size.

What Is the Tolerable Error or the Estimated Effect Size?

To begin consideration of sampling variability in the context of choices, the tolerable error or estimated effect size must be addressed. For descriptive studies, the tolerable error of the estimates must be determined for the variables of greatest interest. The tolerable error relates to the size of the interval around the estimate that is expected, with a specified degree of confidence, to include the population value. For example, an estimate of the percentage of the homeless population that have been released from mental hospitals may need to be within 5% of the actual value. For a candidate in a close election, the tolerable error in a pre-election poll may be 1%. Tolerable error includes an assumption about the likelihood that the true value is contained in the interval.

The estimated size effect must be determined for analytical studies. The estimated size effect is the amount of difference the treatment or independent variable is likely to make in the dependent variable(s). Consider the case of legislation that requires an additional one-year sentence to be added to a sentence when a handgun is used in the commission of a crime. The effect of the legislation is expected to be a 12-month increase in sentences when crimes are committed using a handgun. Research evaluating the actual increase in sentences would need to be sensitive enough to detect a change of sentence length of 12 months. The effect size for a developmental program for 4-year-olds could be estimated in terms of increases in standardized test scores or decreases in the percentage of students held back in the first grade or both. The effect size used in this case could be the minimum amount of change that program sponsors considered to be sufficient to justify costs of the program.

The likely effect size and the tolerable error are used in the calculation of efficient sample sizes. The objective of the researcher is to produce estimates within the limits of tolerable error or to conduct an analytical test that is sensitive enough to detect the estimated effect. Sample size is a principal means by which the researcher can achieve these objectives. But the efficiency of the sampling technique can have considerable impact on the amount of sampling error and the estimate of the desired sample size.

What Type of Sampling Technique Will Be Used?

In Chapter 2, the five basic probability sampling techniques were described:

Simple random sampling
Systematic sampling
Stratified sampling
Cluster sampling
Multistage sampling

While all the techniques are probability techniques, they can each result in sampling bias. The choice of a technique will depend on several factors, including the availability of an adequate sampling frame; the availability of prior information about the target population; the need for greater efficiency; the need to conduct interviews on-site, or alternatively, over the phone; and the location of the target population. However, the choices do not end with the selection of a technique.

Choices branch off independently for each technique. If stratified sampling is chosen, how many strata should be used? If researchers choose cluster sampling, how should the clusters be defined? For multistage samples, can the researcher reduce sampling variability by selecting more of the primary sampling units with fewer secondary units for each primary unit than by selecting fewer primary units with more secondary units for each primary unit? Chapter 4 presents examples of how these choices have been made in practice. Chapter 6 discusses implications of the alternatives.

Will the Probability of Selection Be Equal or Unequal?

Choices about the probability of selection will also affect sampling bias. For simple random sampling, the probability of selecting any individual unit is equal to the sampling fraction or the proportion of the population selected for the sample (n/N). The probability of selecting any unit is equal. For stratified sampling, the probability of selection for any unit is the sampling fraction for the stratum in which the unit is placed. Probabilities using a stratified sampling technique can be either equal or unequal. Multistage samples have the most complex probability of selection calculation. The overall probability of selection is the product of the probabilities of selection in each stage. The calculation must be done separately for each stratum and sampling unit in each stage.

A sample with equal probability of selection is termed a self-weighting sample, indicating that no weights are needed to adjust for unequal probabilities. Unequal probabilities of selection are biased and require weights to be used for estimation and analysis when a design-based approach is being followed. A design-based approach is an approach to estimation and analysis that follows the structure of the design in terms of using weights to compensate for unequal probabilities created by the design. Since the design-based approach to estimation and analysis prevails among sampling practitioners, the design-based approach will be followed throughout this text. Readers interested in an alternative, the model-based approach, are referred to Smith (1976) and Kalton (1986).

How Many Units Will Be Selected for the Sample?

Researchers directly affect the amount of sampling variability in their choice of sample size. Sample size depends on a number of factors. Estimating an efficient sample size is a reasonable place to begin the researcher's decision process. Efficient sample size calculations are ways to estimate the size of the sample needed to fulfill the study objectives once a particular selection technique has been chosen and specified in operational terms. Efficient sample size is computed in one of two ways depending on the nature of the study.

For descriptive studies, the question posed is, what sample size will produce estimates that are precise enough to be useful, given the sampling technique? This relates directly to the choice of the amount of tolerable error. Recall that tolerable error relates solely to the variability due to sampling and does not include the other components of total error. The standard error of the estimate is the measure of sampling variability. Tolerable error is the allowable standard error of the estimate times the t-value selected for the desired probability that the true value will be contained in the interval around the estimate:

$$te = ts_{\bar{x}}$$

where *te* is tolerable error,
$\quad\quad$ *t* is the *t*-value for the desired probability, and
$\quad\quad$ $s_{\bar{x}}$ is the standard error of the estimate.

Tolerable error is the size of one side of the confidence interval, presented earlier ($\pm ts_{\bar{x}}$). Thus, in computing the efficient sample size, the tolerable error is actually one half of the size of the confidence interval that the researcher can tolerate for the study. The tolerable error relates to the amount of precision needed for the estimates.

Based on the formulas presented earlier for the confidence interval, the size of the interval is primarily influenced by three variables: the standard deviation, the sample size, and the t-statistic. To a lesser extent, it can be influenced by the sampling fraction as a result of the finite population correction (FPC). The researcher directly controls only the sample size: to produce an estimate from the sample that is precise enough for the study objectives the researcher can adjust the sample size. But increasing the sample size means increasing the cost of the data collection. Trade-offs between precision and cost are inherent at this juncture.

For a descriptive study, assuming a simple random sample, the sample size calculation is an algebraic transformation of the standard error calculation:

$$n' = s^2/(te/t)^2$$
$$n = n'/(1 + f)$$

where *n'* is the sample size computed in the first step,
$\quad\quad$ *s* is the estimate of the standard deviation,
$\quad\quad$ *te* is the tolerable error,
$\quad\quad$ *t* is the *t*-value for the desired probability level,

        n is the efficient sample size using the finite population
           correction factor, and
        f is the sampling fraction.

Tolerable error, discussed above, is used in this equation. Tolerable error is the allowable standard error of the estimate multiplied by the t-value. In other words, it is the value that will be added to and subtracted from the estimate to form the confidence interval. Therefore, in this equation the tolerable error is divided by the t-value so that it is expressed comparably to the standard error. An example of using this formula for sample size decision is presented in Chapter 4 (see Table 4.6 especially).

The most difficult piece of information to obtain for this formula, considering it is used prior to conducting the actual data collection, is the estimate of the standard deviation. A number of options are available, including prior studies, small pilot studies, and estimates using the range. These options are discussed in Chapter 7.

Power tests are used to compute efficient sample sizes for studies that are primarily analytical. A power test is used to indicate whether a particular sample size is sufficiently sensitive to detect the expected effect (Lipsey, 1989). Rejecting the null hypothesis that there is no effect from the program or treatment depends primarily on the size of the effect and the size of the standard error of the estimate. The larger the standard error or the smaller the effect size, the more difficult it is to reject the null hypothesis. Failure to reject the null hypothesis when it is in fact false is described as a Type II error.

Once again, sample size is the researcher's main tool in obtaining a plausible chance of rejecting the null hypothesis. Lipsey (1989) cites and explains additional methods of avoiding Type II errors, treating the power issue in the overall context of design sensitivity.

While the sample size is the principal means for influencing the precision of the estimate once the design is set, an iterative process can be used to examine the impact on efficient sample size when altering the design, especially the sampling technique. Improved stratification or the selection of more primary sampling units in multistage sampling can improve the efficiency of the design. Of course, these adjustments are also likely to increase costs, but perhaps less than increasing the sample size would.

In addition, other sample size considerations should be brought to bear at this point. For example, will the number of members of subpopulations that are to be described be sufficient in the design using the efficient sample size? When the members of an important subpopulation are a small fraction of the population, it may not be possible to increase the total sample size to a number that would yield a sufficient number of subpopulation members for the analysis. Disproportionate stratification designed to increase the number of subpopulation members or a supplemental sample are possible alternatives. Both have a cost that must be considered, and they may change the efficiency of the design.

Determining the sample size is generally an iterative process. Numerous factors are considered and analyzed that may alter earlier choices. It is important carefully to review the proposed alternatives in terms of total error, changes in the study population definition from using different sampling frames, ability to meet the study objectives, time, and cost. Usually it is beneficial to review each item that has appeared in the framework to examine the impact of the alternative. Impact on other factors such as the cost and interviewer training and follow-up for nonrespondents must also be considered when making the sampling choices.

POSTSAMPLING CHOICES

How Can the Impact of Nonresponse Be Evaluated?

Nonresponse is the lack of valid responses from some members of the sample. Nonresponse can occur when the respondent refuses to answer a particular question or refuses to participate in the survey, or when the respondent cannot be contacted. Nonresponse is one component of nonsampling bias. Nonresponse leads to differences between the study population and the target population. In essence, the population is divided into two subpopulations, responders and nonresponders. The smaller the subpopulation of nonresponders, the less their impact on biasing the results can be (Kalton, 1983). So the best way of dealing with nonresponse is to eliminate it. Fowler (1984) discusses several ways of reducing nonresponse.

Since entirely eliminating nonresponse is unrealistic, the researcher is left having to assess its impact. This can be done by comparing characteristics of the sample with characteristics of the study population, for variables where population values are available. The comparison can help by showing which types of population members are underrepresented. However, the characteristics of the population members for which data are available may not directly relate to variables that are important for the current study. For example, demographic variables such as age, gender, and race are often the only data available for the population. In addition, the data are often out of date and may not reflect the distribution of these characteristics in the current population.

However, where the population data are reasonably timely, it is often useful to weight the sample data to obtain the population proportions and examine the impact of the weighting on the variables of greatest interest for the study. This practice assumes no differences in the responders and nonresponders. It simply compensates for underrepresentation of certain groups. This assumption is not generally borne out.

To test for the amount of bias, a subsample of nonresponders could be randomly selected and intensively followed up to obtain information on important variables for the study. This is sometimes referred to as an attrition study. In the case of mailed surveys, a phone interview follow-up may be used (Dillman & Tarnai, 1988). The data that are obtained can be compared to the data obtained in the original effort to evaluate the potential bias caused by nonresponse. Evaluating nonresponse is discussed in Chapter 8.

Is It Necessary to Weight the Sample Data?

Weighting is usually required to compensate for sampling bias when unequal probabilities result from the researchers' sampling choices. Sometimes weights are needed in some analyses and not in others. For example, a study may have two units of analysis, households and individuals. From each household one individual is selected by a random process to respond. The households are selected with equal probability, so no weights are needed when households are the object of inquiry. Because the probability of selection of a member of the household to be a respondent depends on the number of individuals living in the household, unequal probabilities occur when individuals are the object of inquiry. Thus, weights are needed. The use of weights is discussed in Chapter 8 and examples are presented in Chapter 4.

What Are the Standard Errors for the Study Variables?

Standard errors are important for both descriptive and analytical studies. The precision of the estimates and the sensitivity of hypothesis tests are determined by the standard errors. Standard errors are the measures of sampling variability. Calculating standard errors is complex, since the formulas are different for every statistic and every technique.

Two approaches are used to estimate standard error: a direct method and a more complex method requiring the approximation of the deviations. In practice, the direct method can be used for simple random, systematic, stratified, and cluster samples. Formulas for the direct method can be illustrated by the standard error of the mean calculation for simple random samples that was presented and discussed earlier in the chapter:

$$s_{\bar{x}} = (1 - f)^{1/2} s/(n^{1/2})$$

These formulas are stock features of statistics texts for a variety of statistics assuming that a simple random sample is used.

Other sampling techniques require modifications to the formula using the direct approach. The ratio of the sampling variance ($s_{\bar{x}}{}^2$) for the actual design to the sampling variance, assuming a simple random sample, is called the design effect (Kish, 1965). This ratio shows the extent to which the actual sample design has increased or decreased the sampling variability component of total error. Stratification lowers the sampling error, all other things held constant, and has a design effect less than one. Sampling error and design effect can be further lowered when larger sampling fractions are allocated to strata that have the highest standard deviations.

Cluster sampling has the opposite impact on the design effect: it causes the design effect to exceed one. This occurs because the number of independent choices is the number of clusters in cluster sampling, not the number of units finally selected. The effect is reduced when:

clusters are internally heterogeneous on the important study variables (large standard deviations within the clusters), or

cluster means do not vary.

Since clusters are often geographically defined, increasing the size of the clusters to contain more heterogeneous groupings increases data collection costs. Reducing the sampling variability can also be achieved through stratification of the clusters before selection. This means that the clusters must be placed into strata before selection, and the variables used to define the strata must be available for all clusters.

The calculation of the sampling error for complex, multistage samples using the Taylor approximation of deviations method or some form of repeated replications is only practical with the aid of a computer. In addition, they require that at least two selections be made from each stratum or primary sampling units. Otherwise selections must be combined across strata. Sampling error calculations for complex samples are presented in Chapter 6.

SUMMARY

The challenge of practical sample design is making trade-offs to reduce total error, while keeping study goals and resources in mind. The sampler must act to make choices throughout the sampling process to reduce error. But reducing the error associated with one choice can increase errors from other sources.

Faced with this complex, multidimensional challenge, the researcher must concentrate on reducing total error. Error can arise systematically from bias or occur due to random fluctuation inherent in sampling. Error cannot be entirely eliminated. Reducing error is the practical objective, which can be achieved through careful design.

This chapter has pointed out three components of total error: nonsampling bias, sampling bias, and sampling variability. Each must be addressed through the design. The chapter also presented some basic questions that must be grappled with throughout the design process. Choices to be made at each stage in the process interact with other choices. The next chapter presents four examples of the way choices were made by researchers conducting applied social research.

4

Four Practical Sample Designs

Designing samples requires making choices. Choices made in the sample design and interrelationships between the available alternatives for a design are difficult to understand without actual examples. It is difficult to grasp the significance of trade-offs in the design process without the study context. And often the study consumer cannot resurrect the discarded alternatives, nor fully garner the logic of the design from published accounts that are necessarily oriented toward presenting results.

A major purpose of this book is to stimulate thinking about the range of choices available to a researcher involved in sample design and the implications of those choices for the sample's usefulness in answering the study questions. This chapter is devoted to four case examples. The four cases (a small, nonprobability sample) illustrate a variety of situations faced by researchers, the choices they made, and some of the alternatives ruled out.

Emphasis is placed on studies of statewide scope. Most of the studies with which I have been involved have been statewide studies for both legislative and executive policy-making. From education to highways to corrections, sampling costs and minimizing total error are as important in state studies as in national studies. Advantages of studies at the state or substate level are that they tend to be somewhat less complex than national studies, a useful characteristic for drawing out issues. Also, they present more choices for sampling frames and methods of data collection that are critical factors in integrating practical sampling design into the study process.

The variety of examples is enhanced by the final case which is a national, general-population sample developed by the Survey Research Center of the Institute for Social Research at the University of Michigan. It exemplifies the complexity of developing a sample design for a national data collection effort that utilizes personal interviews. Also, it illustrates the trade-offs made for a sampling design that is developed for multipurpose, multiyear use. However, the description provided herein does not provide enough of the technical underpinnings of sampling to enable the reader to design an area probability sample without guidance from experienced sampling practitioners.

The examples in this section exhibit a variety of different study goals, data collection procedures, and types of populations encountered in prac-

TABLE 4.1
Sample Design Examples

Characteristics	North Carolina Citizen Survey (1977)	Elderly in Florida	Deinstitutionalized Follow-up in Virginia	National SRC Household Survey
Target population	General	Special	Special	General
Data collection	Telephone; mailed surveys	Telephone survey	Administrative records	Personal interviews
Sampling frame	Tax returns; Medicaid rolls	Random digit dialing	Discharge listing	Five, one for each stage
Sampling technique	Stratified	Two-stage stratified	Systematic	Multistage
Probability of selection	Equal-households; unequal-individuals	Unequal by region	Unequal multiple listings	Equal over all (approximately) households
Sample size	1,377	1,647	347	1,485
Weighting	Adults in household	Regional proportions	Number of discharges	None for households

tical research projects. The first is a general population survey developed for the North Carolina Citizen Survey to collect information on opinions and public services. The second case is a survey of the advanced elderly, individuals 75 years of age and older, conducted by telephone in Florida. The third example, a sample designed to follow up on deinstitutionalized mentally ill, was developed in Virginia and relied on administrative records as a data source. See Table 4.1 for an overview of all four examples.

NORTH CAROLINA CITIZEN SURVEY

In 1975, the state of North Carolina began a project to examine the effectiveness of programs in human services as well as transportation and economic development. Measures were developed and data collected over several years concerning health, employment, and the economy. These data were to be used to assess the impact of the policies and programs put into effect in the state. Other items were added to the survey from time to time to assess needs, satisfaction with public services, or to gauge the impact of policy initiatives.

Presampling Choices

Study goals. The study sought to provide reliable estimates of citizen health status, employment, and economic conditions in North Carolina. The estimates were to be compared over time. Thus, the sample procedure was replicated from year to year and was intended to be sensitive enough to detect changes if they occurred. Clearly the study was to produce descriptive information sufficiently accurate and reliable for policy-making purposes: "The resulting data is used by state government agencies in a variety of ways including planning, budget allocation, policymaking and program evaluation" (Williams, 1982b, p. 1).

Data collection method and study population. Decisions related to the data collection method and the study population were tightly intertwined in this example. The survey results were to represent the entire adult population of North Carolina, that is, the target population was the general population of the state. Three alternatives could be considered to achieve this objective: using a random digit dialing sampling method in combination with a telephone survey; using an area sampling technique that assigns a probability of selection to every area of the state and then surveys either all or part of the area's residents; or assembling a list of the population of North Carolina as the sample frame. Each of these alternatives required evaluation of the extent to which the actual study population would be consistent with the definition of the target population.

The first alternative, random digit dialing combined with telephone interviews, is an economical approach. Nonsampling bias is a significant issue with random digit dialing in a substantially rural state where relatively fewer households have phones. At the time the surveys were begun, 87% of the households in the state were estimated to have telephones (U.S. Bureau of the Census, 1975, cited in Grizzle, 1977, p. 3). However, telephone interviews cost less and produced less response bias than personal interviews with more threatening questions. Also, they yield relatively high interview completion rates (Bradburn & Sudman, 1980). Low nonresponse could be further improved by using an intensive follow-up procedure (Fowler, 1984).

Area probability sampling, the second alternative, is a complex sampling procedure that usually involves multistage sampling of smaller and smaller geographic units. The final stage of area probability sampling is the selection of a household from which a respondent is selected. Area probability sampling is generally used in conjunction with personal interviews. Also, area probability sampling usually increases the sampling variability because of the tendency for individuals in the same geographic area to share similar traits.

To obtain the economy and high response rate of telephone interviews, when possible, and avoid the bias of excluding households without phones, the development of a listing of North Carolina residents was a preferable alternative to random digit dialing or area probability sampling. No single listing of residents was comprehensive enough to use as the sampling frame. Household tapes from the 1970 census, listings in telephone directories, listings of households connected to city water lines, and city directories were not sufficiently comprehensive to reduce the nonsampling bias to a tolerable level (Grizzle, 1977, p. 2). However, the research staff found that by combining the list of 1975 North Carolina income tax returns, which included heads of households, and the list of North Carolinians eligible for Medicaid assistance in 1975, an estimated 96% of the households estimated for North Carolina were included in the sampling frame (Grizzle, 1977, p. 3). In 1981, the coverage of the households by the sampling frame was estimated to be 94%.

The lists for the sampling frame provided names and addresses for the study population. To reduce expense, telephone numbers were obtained for the sample, and telephone interviews were used as the primary data collection method. The telephone interviews were replaced by personal interviews when the selected household did not have a listed telephone number or could not be reached by phone. Of completed interviews, 78% were done by telephone, and the remainder were personal interviews.

Sampling Choices

The study population was defined as individuals within the households that filed 1975 income tax returns in North Carolina or were eligible for Medicaid assistance, including recipients of Aid to Families with Dependent Children, Supplemental Social Security, and the medically needy. These two lists covered two large segments of the population of North Carolina since many of the medically needy do not file tax returns.

The sampling technique employed was a stratified approach using each list as a separate stratum. In the initial sample, a simple random sample was selected from each stratum maintaining the population proportions. Thus, the household sample used equal probability of selection and was selfweighting, 89% from the tax list and 11% from the Medicaid list. Later samples increased the proportion of the sample from the Medicaid list because the nonresponse rate from that list was higher than that from the tax list. The adjustment of the proportions from the Medicaid list produced the 13.5% in the actual respondents that corresponded to the proportion that the list contained of the total households (Williams, 1982b, p. 9).

The sample size target was set at approximately 1,400 respondents. Based on the selection of one respondent from each household and a probable 25% nonresponse and ineligible rate (e.g., living in another state but filing a tax return in North Carolina), approximately 1,800 to 2,000 households were sampled from the lists. The formula for calculating the number of households needed to achieve the desired sample size is:

$$n' = n \, / \, (1 \, - \, nr \, - \, i)$$

where n is the target for the final sample size,
n' is the size of the sample taken from the list,
nr is the estimated proportion of nonresponses, and
i is the estimated proportion of ineligibles on list.

The sampling variability associated with this sample design and size can be conveniently approximated using the simple random sample formula for proportions:

$$s_p = (p(1 \, - \, p)/n)^{\frac{1}{2}}$$

This formula is used to estimate the sampling variability; for example, if 69% of the sample exhibited a particular characteristic, the standard error would be: $s_p = (69)(31)/1,377)^{\frac{1}{2}} = (2,139/1,377)^{\frac{1}{2}} = 1.25$. The formula for stratified samples, which would yield a more precise estimate, is given in Chapter 6. However, with only two strata the approximation is adequate. Table 4.2 shows the standard error estimate and the 95% confidence interval for several variables in the 1981 fall survey that were computed after the data were collected.

The standard errors in Table 4.2 show that larger standard errors are associated with proportions that are closer to .50. A finding of interest to health policymakers is that 85% of the North Carolinians were estimated to use doctors' offices as the main source of health care. The researchers were 95% confident that as many as 87% or as few as 83% of the state's residents used doctors' offices in this way.

The subpopulation of those who moved to North Carolina, rather than natives, showed a higher standard error, because of the smaller number in that particular subsample (459). The standard error was nearly twice as large (2.3) for this subpopulation. In the example presented, the proportion of those who have moved to North Carolina within the last 10 years is estimated to be 42%. The study users can be 95% confident that between

TABLE 4.2

Proportions, Standard Errors, and Confidence Intervals for
North Carolina Citizen Survey

			95% Interval	
Variable	Proportion	s_p	p greater than	p less than
n = 1,377				
Employment in household	.69	.0125	.666	.714
Income from public source in household	.48	.0135	.454	.506
Job satisfaction	.53	.0134	.504	.556
Likely to lose job within one year	.16	.0099	.141	.179
Excellent health	.86	.0093	.842	.878
Doctor's office main source of health care	.85	.0096	.831	.869
n = 459				
Moved to North Carolina within last 10 years	.42	.0230	.375	.465

37% and 47% of the subpopulation that has moved to North Carolina moved there within the last 10 years.

Postsampling Choices

Weighting responses is needed in this study to obtain estimates of the responses representing individuals rather than households. Households were selected with equal probability from the list. The probability that an individual would be selected as a respondent would depend on the number of eligible respondents in the household. For example, the respondent selected in a one-person household would be four times as likely to be selected as the respondent in a household with four eligible respondents. The probability of selection is the reciprocal of the number of eligible respondents in the household. The weights are normally constructed using the following formula:

$$w = e_i(n/\Sigma e)$$

where w is the weight,

e_i is the number of eligibles in the household, and

n is the sample size.

For example, a total sample size of 1,377 and a total pool of 4,022 eligibles would yield a factor ($n/\Sigma e$) of .342. This factor is multiplied by the number of eligibles in a particular household to produce the weights to adjust for sampling bias. A household with one member would have a weight of .342; the member selected in a four-person household would have a weight of 1.369. The probability of selection is inversely proportional to the weight. The effect of the $n/\Sigma e$ factor, .342 in this case, is to maintain the total sample size equal to the sum of the weights, a convenience for the computation of tests of significance.

The logic of the weighting is based upon the number of individuals being represented by the respondent. The single-member household represents one individual within that household. The individual selected as the respondent in the four-person household represents four individuals. Therefore, the respondent in the four-person household requires four times as much weight as the one-person household ($1.369/.342 = 4$).

The data from the survey have been carefully reported to inform the reader of the possible selection bias in the survey results. Table 4.3 compares the estimates from the sample in various categories for which external data were available with population data. The author of the report highlights summarized the representativeness of the sample this way: "Overall, the distribution of key demographic characteristics of the Fall 1982 Citizen Survey sample . . . corresponds closely to independent statewide estimates. Minor discrepancies were noted in age, sex, income and education" (Williams, 1982b, p. 77). The comparisons were closer in the 1982 survey than in the 1981 survey, which is at least partially attributable to the oversampling of the Medicaid list noted earlier.

SURVEY OF THE FRAIL ELDERLY IN FLORIDA

Frail elderly, defined as individuals 75 years of age and older, are a sizable and growing portion of the population in Florida. These individuals are those most likely to require services supported through Medicaid, including long-term care in a nursing home. To facilitate planning for the services needed by these individuals and to examine the feasibility of alternatives to residential care, information on the target population is needed by state officials.

TABLE 4.3

Demographic Characteristics of North Carolina Citizen Survey Respondents:
Comparison of Percentages for Fall 1982 with External Data Source

Demographic Characteristics	External Estimate	NCC Fall 1982	
		Weighted	Unweighted
Age			
18-29	31.4	26.0	22.9
30-49	34.1	38.7	39.4
50-64	20.3	22.6	22.6
65 and over	14.3	12.8	15.1
Sex			
Male	48.6	44.6	42.9
Female	51.5	55.4	57.1
Race			
White	78.1	76.5	78.8
Nonwhite	21.9	23.5	21.2
Household income			
$4,000 or less	10.7	5.9	7.6
$4,001-8,000	11.5	10.5	12.1
$8,001-12,000	15.9	13.6	14.3
$12,001-20,000	21.9	30.4	29.9
Over $20,000	40.1	39.6	36.0
Schooling			
8 years and under	18.3	15.4	15.9
Some high school	18.0	16.5	16.0
High school graduate	35.4	40.1	39.0
Some college	13.5	15.4	15.8
College graduate	14.8	12.7	13.3
Region			
Mountain	14.7	15.8	15.3
Piedmont	53.7	54.0	55.0
Coastal Plain	21.5	20.4	19.7
Coast	10.2	9.7	10.0

SOURCE: Williams, 1982b.

Presampling Choices

Study goals. In 1984, state officials decided that a needs assessment of
the frail elderly in Florida was required to update previous needs assessments
of the elderly conducted in 1977 and 1980. The needs assessment was to
be used in conjunction with in-depth studies of the long-term care programs
that were currently available in the state. The study's authors point out that

the other studies, "provide in-depth descriptions and analyses of the elderly served by various HRS [Health and Rehabilitative Services] programs—
their medical problems, who helps them, sources of income, and the like.
These data raise inevitable questions such as, how do program clients compare to those who are not receiving services? What is the need in the larger
population for services such as Adult Foster Care or Homemaker Services?"
(Stutzman, 1985, p. 3).

The principal investigator for the study was Mary Stutzman and the
source of the material presented for this example was the report, *Florida's
75+ Population: A Baseline Data Sourcebook* (1985). Stutzman (p. 16)
outlines the two major study objectives as:

Gather demographic, health, and services data for the 75+ population.

Evaluate the feasibility of gathering data for the 75+ population using a telephone
survey.

The variables, which were to be used for primarily descriptive purposes,
were conceptualized in five principal categories:

Demographic characteristics
General health
Functional abilities and assistance
Services and social supports
Future care demands

Data collection method. One of the study objectives was to pioneer the
use of telephone interviews for the 75+ population. Program personnel
held the belief that the elderly would not agree to participate in telephone
interviews. Previous needs assessments were done using in-person interviews. However, cost was a primary consideration for this study. Travel
costs and interview costs for personal interviews, the alternative method
considered, are much higher than costs to conduct telephone interviews.
The previous needs assessments were done in very restricted locations and
spread over a number of years due to cost constraints.

The cost of personal interviews can be especially prohibitive when the
target population only represents a small fraction of the total population
(6.5% in this case) and no list is available. Less than 65 households out
of 1,000 contacted would have an advanced elderly residing there. Many
contacted households would be screened out of the sample because no eligible individual resided there, greatly increasing the time and transportation
costs of the study. The cost can be decreased when a cluster or multistage

sample is used with the personal interviews. However, clustering increases the sampling variability. Therefore, to obtain the same sampling variability with the clustering, a larger number of interviews must be obtained. Sudman presented a way to improve the efficiency of a cluster sample design to be used in conjunction with personal interviews when screening for rare populations (1976). However, in a situation where telephone interviews are a viable option and cost is an important factor, the telephone method is worth exploring.

Because of costs, the data collection alternatives boiled down to the use of a client listing and personal interviews or a telephone survey with a screening question to identify the presence in the household of a 75-or-older resident. Choosing the first alternative has a decidedly negative impact on nonsampling bias, because the unserved, advanced elderly population is excluded.

Sampling Choices

Population choices. The target population for the study was the 75-and-older population of Florida. The possibility of using telephone interviews opened up three options for obtaining a sampling frame: obtaining a list of the 75+ population; obtaining a list of the general population from which the 75+ population could be screened; or using random digit dialing.

The only conceivable list of the 75+ population was the list of those currently receiving services from HRS. Since this would reproduce the nonsampling bias of the other studies and forgo the opportunity to answer the type of questions posed above, use of this list was dropped. The second conceivable option, using a general population list, was eliminated because of the problems with selection bias of lists obtainable on a statewide basis. General population listings adequate for use as a sampling frame are usually not available on a national, state, or even local basis (Hess, 1985). For example, telephone books omit unlisted and recently added numbers as well as households without telephones. Using telephone books as sampling frames would have resulted in underrepresenting the very poor, the very wealthy, and the mobile parts of the population. The North Carolina example presented above was a relatively rare, but creative, example because researchers in many states are prohibited from obtaining similar lists of clients and lists from tax returns.

Random digit dialing constituted the only viable choice for use as a sampling frame, an implicit sampling frame in this case. The study population became households with a telephone within which a person 75+ resided. The study population has a bias to the extent that the 75+ individuals live in households without phones or that the presence of a 75+ resident was not acknowledged by the individual answering the phone.

Sampling techniques. For selecting the sample, stratified selection was combined with a two-stage approach to random digit dialing developed by Waksberg (1978). To allow regional comparisons for the 11 HRS districts, researchers opted to allocate a minimum of 100 cases to each district. The other cases were distributed in proportion to the 75+ population estimates in the 1980 census (Stutzman, 1985). The disproportionate stratified sampling approach mandated the use of weights to compensate for the unequal probability of selection.

Waksberg developed a two-stage approach to use with random digit dialing principally to reduce the number of phone calls to nonresidential numbers, which were excluded from the study (1978, p. 40). Waksberg estimated that only 20% of the numbers generated in a simple random digit dialing process are assigned to households (1978). The method involves listing the area code, the working prefix numbers, and all possible combinations of the next two digits of the phone numbers in the region of interest. Eight-digit numbers are sampled at random from the list and the final two digits are chosen randomly. This number is used to attempt an interview. If it is a residential number, an interview is completed and the first eight digits are used as a primary sampling unit. Those eight digits are used with a randomly selected pair of final digits until a set number of households is reached. The process is repeated until the desired sample size is obtained. The method is set forth in operational detail in Lavrakas (1986).

This process was used to obtain 1,647 interviews. Researchers established a target of 1,500 interviews. "In order to have a 3 to 4 percent sampling error for the entire state of Florida descriptions and estimates (95% level of confidence), a sample size of approximately 1,500 was needed" (Stutzman, 1985, p. 24). To produce the 1,647 interviews, 71,896 phone calls were made to a total of 38,866 (15,687 + 23,179) phone numbers. Of this total, 21,129 (10,646 + 10,483) nonhousehold numbers and 15,526 (4,430 + 11,096) households that did not indicate 75+ residents were called. (See Figure 4.1 for a more detailed breakdown of phone numbers selected and the Waksberg method.)

Postsampling Choices

Two sets of weights were needed to compensate for the processes that produced unequal probability of selection. First, the stratification by region was disproportionate. Table 4.4 shows the targeted number of interviews, completed interviews, and weighted cases by region. The second set of

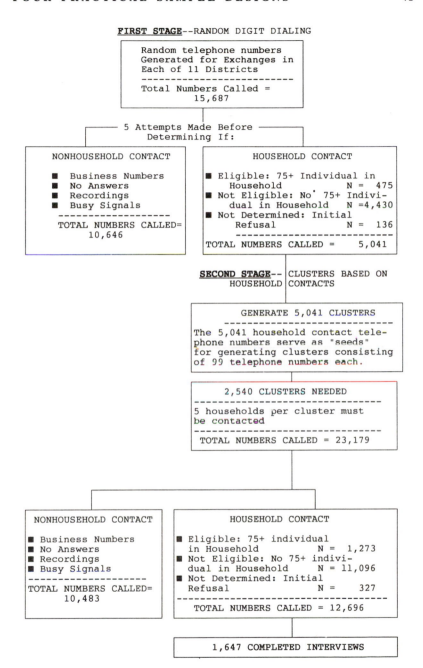

Figure 4.1. Surveying the 75 and Older Population: The Sampling Strategy
SOURCE: Stutzman, 1985.

TABLE 4.4
Frail Elderly Survey: Weighted Cases

District	Population of Frail Elderly		Actual Sample Data		Expected Number in Sample	Weight[2]
	Population[1]	Percent	Completed Interviews	Percentage of Sample		
1	12,471	2.0	113	6.9	33	0.289
2	17,197	2.7	111	6.7	45	0.406
3	36,857	5.9	143	8.7	96	0.675
4	49,395	7.9	107	6.5	129	1.209
5	106,666	17.0	252	15.3	279	1.108
6	66,425	10.6	142	8.6	174	1.225
7	40,090	6.4	117	7.1	105	0.897
8	50,088	8.0	108	6.6	131	1.214
9	62,525	9.9	135	8.2	164	1.213
10	79,081	12.6	174	10.6	207	1.190
11	108,291	17.2	245	14.9	284	1.157
Total	629,086	100.2	1,647	100.1	1,647	

[1]SOURCE: U.S. Bureau of the Census

$$[2]\text{Weight} = \frac{\text{Expected Number in Sample}}{\text{Actual Number in Sample}}$$

where, Expected Number in Sample = (% Population) × (Total Sample Size), and

$$\% \text{ Population} = \frac{\text{Number of 75+ in District}}{\text{Total 75+ in State}}$$

weights were needed to compensate for the respondent selection process when more than one eligible individual resided in the sampled household. The "cluster effect" is the same as with the North Carolina Citizen Survey and the formula for the weights is the same.

The potential bias resulting from nonresponse as well as other sources can also be evaluated at this point. While comparisons with independent sources of information for the target population cannot establish that no selection bias is present, it can point out obvious problems (Table 4.5).

In this case, there were no obvious problems with the population characteristics available. Males, whites, and those over 79 were slightly overrepresented in this sample. Allowing for the 3%–4% sampling error, the sample proportions and the census proportions are insufficiently different to require an additional poststratification weighting.

TABLE 4.5
Sample and Population Characteristics: A Comparison
Frail Elderly in Forida

Characteristics	Sample	Official Census Projections for 1985
Sex		
Male	41.4%	40.0%
Female	58.6%	60.0%
Ethnicity		
White	86.7%	88.9%
Black	7.0%	5.3%
Hispanic	5.9%	5.4%
Age		
75-79	46.7%	50.4%
80-84	30.6%	29.5%
85+	22.8%	20.1%

SOURCE: 1985 census projections and 1980 census. General Population Characteristics: Florida (PC80-1B41: Table 24), and Stutzman, 1985.

DEINSTITUTIONALIZED MENTALLY ILL IN VIRGINIA

In the mid-1980s national attention focused on the homeless and the impact of the policy of deinstitutionalizing the mentally ill on the growing numbers of homeless, particularly street people. A central issue in understanding the contribution of deinstitutionalization to the homeless population involved understanding the linkage between institutions and the provision of services in communities. In 1982, the Virginia legislature requested technical assistance and information on the deinstitutionalized. The request was a follow-up on a 1979 study by the Joint Legislative Audit and Review Commission. The legislators intended to use the statistical information as well as conduct hearings and gather data from a wide range of individuals familiar with the problem.

Presampling Choices

Study goals. The primary goal of the study was to evaluate the deinstitutionalization of mentally ill individuals from the state's mental health hospitals and monitor the provision of services in the community.

One specific goal of the study was to estimate the impact of predischarge planning practices used by the institutions prior to discharging a client into the community (Joint Legislative Audit and Review Commission, 1986). The objective of planning was to facilitate transfer between hospital services and community services. For example, a predischarge conference attended by a service provider or case manager that would be responsible for treatment of the discharged client was one practice to be evaluated.

The researchers wanted to test the relationships between types of patients and discharge procedures with the initiation and maintenance of community-based services. Conceptually, this made the target population definition and data collection method selection straightforward. The target population was the deinstitutionalized patients who had resided in the state's mental health hospitals. The data could be collected from records held by community service providers and the hospitals.

Operationalizing the population definition and the data collection method was difficult. The population definition was complicated by the policy environment in three ways:

(1) The "revolving" door of mental health care means that an individual can be admitted and discharged several times from a hospital. Thus, a list of discharges represented a "transaction" point in the process. Individuals could be involved in several transactions, thereby showing up on the list several times and increasing their probability of selection.

(2) Predischarge procedures had changed in July 1984, a few months prior to the study. Selecting individuals discharged under the old procedure would not evaluate the current practices.

(3) Obtaining data from the community constituted a follow-up. Individuals must be in the community from four months to a year to determine if they obtain community services and if they have a stable relationship with the service provider.

These three issues were resolved by developing a sampling frame consisting of all discharges from the state's mental hospitals between September 1 and October 31, 1984. The September 1 date allowed sufficient time for the new discharge procedures to be implemented. The October 31 date obtained: (1) enough discharges to sample; (2) at least four months of data following the discharge of each client; (3) only 4 clients out of the 350 sampled with multiple listings indicating more than one discharge.

Data collection. Data collection consisted of extracting information from the hospital- and community-based records for each client. To obtain a reasonably complete picture of the client's involvement with the public mental health system, the client history between February 1, 1983, and February 1, 1985, was collected. Special emphasis was placed on the particular release that occurred during the sample period, and most of the data collected was specific to that release and the institutionalization prior to the release.

Data collection involving records spanning two years at multiple sites involved great expense. Maintaining the confidentiality of the records increased the expense. In this case, the time and cost involved in intensive administrative record review, combined with the need to provide the legislature with technical assistance, set constraints on the size of the sample.

Sampling Choices

In working through the definition of the population and method of data collection, several imperatives were placed on the sampling choices. The operational definition of the study population had been established, but its implications for sampling bias had not been fully explored. The primary concern was whether discharges from September and October had any potentially confounding seasonal relationships. An examination of the number of discharges showed no obvious seasonal patterns, though fluctuations were evidenced. Further, independent experts and practitioners did not identify any expected seasonal patterns. Discharges were believed to be influenced by other factors in the system, such as space in the hospitals and availability of community services. These were not characterized as either seasonal or cyclical.

Other sampling choices were significantly constrained by the circumstances:

(1) Sample size was a product of cost and time rather than an estimate of the tolerable error or power required. Table 4.6 shows some estimates of the sampling errors expected for proportions of the population and a subpopulation. Cognizance of threats of low statistical power were to be important in analyzing instances where expected relationships were not found in the data. A sample size of 350 was selected as the maximum number feasible. Table 4.6 shows the impact of three sample sizes on the size of the confidence intervals. The maximum confidence interval occurs with the proportion .5 and the size of the interval decreases with more extreme proportions.

(2) The sampling frame contained no information that could be used to stratify the clients other than the hospital from which they had been discharged. Implicit stratification was used by arranging the list by hospital and selecting the sample systematically. This produced an equal probability sample of discharges exactly proportionate to the number of discharges by hospital.

(3) The equal probability sample of discharges was an unequal probability sample of clients to the extent that some clients had multiple discharges during the period. Only four clients selected had more than one discharge, two in each case.

TABLE 4.6

Deinstitutionalized Mentally Ill in Virginia.
95% Confidence Intervals for Proportions

| Proportion | *Overall Population Estimate* | | |
		Sample Size	
$p (1 - p)$	*300*	*400*	*500*
.10-.90	± .03	± .03	± .03
.30-.70	± .05	± .04	± .04
.50-.50	± .06	± .05	± .04

| Proportion of Dropouts | | *Subpopulation of Dropouts[1]* | |
		Subsample Size Based on Overall Sample Size	
p $(1 - p)$	*300*	*400*	*500*
.20 .80	60 (±.13)	80 (±.11)	100 (±.10)
.30 .70	90 (±.10)	120 (±.09)	150 ±.08)
.40 .60	120 (±.09)	160 (±.08)	200 (±.07)
.50 .50	150 (±.08)	200 (±.07)	250 (±.06)

[1]Subsample size and confidence interval in parentheses for each cell assuming worst-case proportion of .5. Confidence intervals: $1.96([p][1 - p]/n)^{1/2}$.
SOURCE: Joint Legislative Audit and Review Commission staff analysis.

Postsampling Choices

Nonresponse and the concomitant problem of nonsampling bias are generally the most intractable postsampling issues. However, in this case nonresponse was a nonissue. Data was obtained on 347 of the 350 clients in the sample. The relatively small sample size, the use of legally required records, and intensive follow-up procedures removed almost all nonresponse. This was a unique and significant point. The legislative mandate for this study provided access to data and extraordinary cooperation of field personnel in collecting data. Deinstitutionalized clients are an extremely difficult group about which to obtain follow-up data. It would have been easy to hypothesize that the nonresponse group would have exhibited different characteristics. This was, however, not a factor in the analysis of the sample data. Weighting was another potential postsampling issue. The sample was an equal probability sample of discharges and an unequal

TABLE 4.7

Deinstitutionalized Mentally Ill in Virginia

$(n = 347)$

Demographics	Proportion	s_p	95% Confidence Interval greater than:	less than:
Male	.58	.03	.53	.63
White	.68	.03	.63	.73
Single	.82	.02	.78	.86
Unemployed when admitted	.85	.02	.81	.89
Mental health status after discharge				
Required medication	.78	.02	.74	.82
Required supervised living situation	.73	.02	.68	.78
Made contact with community services	.63	.03	.58	.68
Maintained contact with community services for at least four months	.40	.03	.35	.45
Subpopulation:				
Not making contact with community service providers	.37	.03	.32	.42
	$n = 127$			
Moved, received private services, or returned to correctional setting	.39	.04	.31	.47
Refused services	.25	.04	.17	.33
No contact	.30	.04	.22	.38

SOURCE: Rog and Henry, 1986.

probability sample of clients. Weighting for the paucity (four cases) of un-equal probability clients resulted in no detectable differences in the data analysis. Therefore, weights were omitted in the analysis, shown in Table 4.7.

SURVEY RESEARCH CENTER'S NATIONAL HOUSEHOLD SAMPLE

In the early 1970s, the Survey Research Center (SRC) affiliated with the Institute for Social Research at the University of Michigan undertook revision of their national sample design. The sample was to be used for several studies requiring personal interviews. The sample design has been used for two to four studies per year between 1972 and 1980, including the National Election Studies and surveys of consumer finances, attitudes, and behaviors (Hess, 1985, p. 19).

Presampling Choices

Study goals. The major purpose of the 1970 revision of the national sample was to provide a flexible sample of counties that would allow a probability selection of either households or the adult population of the 48 conterminous states and the District of Columbia. In this case the sample was not being designed for a single data collection effort. The selection of counties and cities, towns, and rural areas was to last for a decade of studies. Irene Hess had primary responsibility for the sampling work of the Survey Research Center (SRC) during the time the revision was undertaken and the description here of this example relies on her book *Sampling for Social Surveys, 1947-1980.*

A related goal of the sample design was to provide an equal probability of selection for the household studies. Equal probability of selection would simplify the analysis of the data by eliminating weights to compensate for unequal probability of selection. This feature is especially desirable in the case of the SRC's work because the data are made available and used by numerous researchers and instructors across the country. Equal probability of selection greatly enhances the ease of use of the data.

The sample design was to provide approximately 3,000 interviews with heads of spending units, which because of disproportionate selection and screening required an initial 5,000 to 6,000 households (Hess, 1985, p. 34). The 5,000 to 6,000 units were considered a maximum needed for the design based on the type of statistical procedures and the variables to be analyzed in the multiple studies using the sample design. Procedures were developed to reduce that number when less precision would suffice.

Another goal of the 1970 revision was to maintain continuity, to the extent possible, with the data series begun in the late 1940s, which used the national sample of households.

Data collection. Another goal was necessitated by using personal interviews as the data collection method, that is, the practical consideration of maintaining a staff of interviewers who could accomplish a nationwide data collection effort in six to eight weeks several times each year in an economical manner. Personal interviews, conducted on a national basis, require a staff of trained interviewers for accurate data collection and a sampling procedure that limits travel time. The limit on travel time is especially important when the study design requires screening the household residents, the selection of a specific resident, and follow-up visits.

Study population. The target population for a national sample of households is the adult population of the United States. The sample can be used as a sample of households or a sample of individuals. However, practical aspects of sampling have placed limits on the study population. First, the residents of Alaska and Hawaii are not included in the design. Together their population is less than 1% of the U.S. population. The difficulty of maintaining interviewers for such small segments of the population outweighed the impact of excluding them. Second, the population residing on military bases are excluded because of the paucity of information on the number residing in particular locations. Third, institutional living units, including situations as diverse as prisons, college dorms, and homes for adults, are excluded from the study population (Hess, 1985, p. 24). Finally, screens were often used during the initial part of the interview to further screen the study population, generally to match the target population. For example, the National Election Studies screened out individuals who were not citizens of the United States and those below the voting age. When the screens turned up more than one household member in the target population, an objective procedure was utilized to make the selection of an individual a probability selection rather than a haphazard selection based on who happens to be available or the discretion of the interviewer.

Sampling Choices

The range of choices for national samples of individuals and households is limited by the fact that no register or listing of the target population is available. Furthermore, a list that does not exclude large portions of the population cannot be constructed without insurmountable expense. Therefore, a multistage area probability sample is required to obtain the benefits of a probability sample, given the concern of cost and the need for face-to-face interviews.

The only commonly used alternative to a multistage sample involves combining random digit dialing with telephone interviews. Bradburn and Sudman (1980) discuss the relative validity of administering an instrument over the phone as opposed to personal interviews or mailed questionnaires. Lavrakas (1986) discusses the potential bias of excluding parts of the target population through phone surveys and the practicalities of implementing the process.

The design for household selection includes five stages, shown in Table 4.8. In the first stage, 74 Standard Metropolitan Statistical Areas (SMSAs),

TABLE 4.8

Stages in the National Household Studies Sample

State	Units	Brief Description
1	Counties, SMSAs, and SCAs[1]	2,700 units were placed in 74 strata; 10 largest SMSAs and SCAs selected with certainty; one primary unit selected from 64 other strata.
2	Cities, towns, and rural areas	3-10 units selected from each of the 74 primary units (average of 5); stratified by size.
3	Blocks in cities and towns; chunks in rural areas	Minimum of 3 units selected from 370 secondary units.
4	Clusters expected to contain 4 households	Number of selections determined by overall probability of selection, results in equal probability of cluster selection.
5	Households	All or part of the 4 expected households were selected. Equal probability of selection maintained.
6	Eligible individual	Fixed, objective selection mechanism resulted in unequal probability of selection.

[1]SMSAs—standard metropolitan statistical area; SCAs—standard consolidated area.

Standard Consolidated Areas (SCAs), or counties, where counties lie outside SMSAs and SCAs, were selected. In the second stage, 3 to 10 cities, towns, or rural areas were selected from the 74 primary sampling units. The third stage included the selection of blocks in cities and towns and "chunks" or small geographic units in counties. Clusters were then selected, and finally households were selected from the clusters.

An additional stage is added for the studies that use the individual as the unit of analysis, which involves choosing the respondent from the eligible respondents in the household. Chapter 5 presents alternative methods of selecting the respondent for the household. When more than one member of the household is eligible for participation in the survey, the selection affects the overall probability of selection for the survey. This is analogous to a situation where the sampling frame consists of a listing of clusters or groups of individuals that are the units of analysis for the study. The impact on the equal probability of selection can be compensated for, when necessary, by weighting.

Sample size, as the previous chapter illustrates, has a major impact on the sampling variability and the precision of the estimates calculated from sample data. Calculations have been devised that allow the researcher to minimize the sample size for a fixed cost or minimize the cost for a fixed level of precision (Kish, 1965; Sudman, 1976). The multiple surveys for which this sample design would be developed placed three practical constraints on establishing the size of the sample.

First, the studies using the design had vastly different subjects of interest and, therefore, different variables of interest and analytical techniques. To allow flexibility for different study goals, it is not desirable to fix the sample size for all studies. Second, the population values (i.e., the population standard deviation and cost of interview estimates) required for a minimization solution in each of the various studies are usually unknown since the research was largely exploratory, according to Hess (1985). Finally, and perhaps most importantly, Hess explicitly recognized the trade-off between sampling and nonsampling error in evaluating the sample size question:

> Since many of the Center's household surveys addressed relatively new areas of research and involved long and intensive interviews that were frequently subject to large nonsampling errors, the sample sizes were small, usually from 1,000 to 3,000 interviews from as many households. Increasing sample size in order to reduce sampling error in new and exploratory research generally is misplaced effort because the total error to which surveys are subject is often dominated by the nonsampling error terms. (p. 24)

Postsampling Choices

Error resulting from the study design must be examined to ascertain the extent to which validity problems have occurred. Unfortunately, estimating the actual impact of nonsampling errors is a more qualitative than quantitative exercise. And the estimation of sampling variability of the sample is less than exact, especially for complex samples.

Nonsampling bias of the design is the most likely source of error. Three components of nonsampling bias are observable in the sample design. First, a number of households in the target population are not covered in the sample design, when compared to the Census Bureau's Current Population reports. The 4%-9% difference in the survey estimates and census data cannot be reconciled by known omissions including households in Alaska and Hawaii and those on military reservations (Hess, 1985, p. 240).

Second, the number of individuals within a household is underreported. In most cases where independent estimates are available, the younger age categories are underrepresented in the national household surveys (Hess, 1985, pp. 246-257). The SRC interviewers are instructed to omit any family members residing in college dorms, on military bases, and in some facilities for the elderly from the list of household residents. This as well as intentional underreporting by respondents contributes to the under-reporting within households.

Nonresponse is the final component of nonsampling bias. While personal interviews have a lower rate of refusal than mail surveys, the refusal rate for the national sample of households is significant. The nonresponse rate for selected SRC samples in the 1970s averaged 25.2% (Hess, 1985, p. 59). The nonresponse is higher in metropolitan areas than in non-metropolitan areas, and it is much higher in the central cities within metropolitan areas.

Sampling variability. An overall estimate of the sampling variability for the national household sample is difficult to calculate for two reasons. The sample is actually several different samples taken over the course of the decade of the 1970s, each of which would require a separate although related calculation of sampling variability. In addition, sampling variability is a function of the estimator as well as the sample design. Thus, the sampling variability depends on the variable(s) under study and the statistical technique.

Furthermore, the formulas for simple random samples shown in the previous chapter do not necessarily yield accurate results for more complex designs such as the national household survey. The use of area sampling increases the sampling variability because individuals within the areas sampled tend to share common characteristics (Kish, 1965). But the degree of homogeneity depends on the actual similarities found within the sampled areas. The inflation of the standard error that occurs due to the area sampling technique is partially offset by stratification. Stratification, as will be shown in Chapter 6, decreases sampling variability, principally by making the selections more heterogeneous.

Stuart, after examining the relationship between the sampling variability in simple and more complex samples states, "A rough rule based on these results is to multiply the unrestricted random sampling error by 1.25 or 1.50. . . . It [the rough rule] may nevertheless be of value as a guide if a considerable volume of data is under survey" (1963, p. 89).

More precise calculations of the sampling variability for complex samples have been devised and are especially useful for calculating the sampling variability for more complex statistics, such as regression coefficients. One method, balanced repeated replications, involves obtaining data on sub-samples that are repeated applications of the sample design (Sudman, 1976, p. 178). The subsample estimates are combined to calculate the overall estimates. The sampling variability is calculated by omitting a subsample and determining the variability of the remaining combined subsamples. However, the selection of repeated subsamples lowers the number of strata that can be used in the design. Fewer strata reduce the efficiency of the design and, all other things being equal, increase the sampling variability.

Other methods of estimating sampling variability have developed using the concept of repetitions without the strict design requirements of the balanced repeated replications method. One method, the half sample repeated replication method, pairs observations in strata that maintain the original design structure as closely as possible. Repeatedly, half samples of the original sample are selected independently choosing one observation from each pair. The sampling variability is the average of the sum of the differences between the full sample estimate and the half sample estimates.

Another method is called jackknifing. This method also involves the concept of replication, but only one primary sampling unit is dropped at a time. By iteratively dropping a primary sampling unit from a stratum, reweighting the other unit in the stratum, and computing the statistics, the contribution of the stratum to the sampling variability can be estimated. The variability can be summed across all strata to estimate the overall sampling variability. Obviously, standard error estimates requiring repeated calculation require computer software programs.

SUMMARY

The four examples presented in this chapter illustrate the interplay between overall study goals, the data collection method, the definition of the population, and the choices for the sample design. The impact of these choices on postsampling choices and procedures is evident in the examples. These four sample designs point out the practical side of developing sample designs in different situations. Creative sampling solutions facilitated the realization of research goals. These solutions have often been the product of developments in probability theory and sampling theory such as the Waksburg method and the ways of estimating sampling variability. But in the development of sampling techniques and practices, concerns for validity of the findings and reduction of uncertainty are combined with the practical concerns for data collection operations and cost in the domain of the sample design. These two fundamental concerns cause the creative tension that has contributed to each design presented in this section.

5

Sampling Frames

Sampling choices, beginning with choosing a sampling frame, are made by generating, comparing, and evaluating the implications of alternative choices. However, this process is decidedly nonlinear. As this chapter will highlight, decisions concerning sampling choices can affect the ability to carry out choices made earlier. Choices also constrain alternatives to be selected later. The process is iterative.

Decisions about the sampling frame influence the amount of total error resulting from the practical sampling design. Consistency of the fit between the target population and sampling frame lessens nonsampling bias and, thereby, lessens total error. Certain frame choices are exclusive to particular sampling techniques to be used. Thus, while this chapter and the next two present issues in choosing sampling frames, sampling techniques, and sample size separately, they are in fact interrelated.

Sampling frame choices must be evaluated by several criteria:

- Total error including nonsampling bias and sampling variability
- Cost
- Feasibility
- Constraints on other choices

It is useful to begin the discussion of sampling frame alternatives by first making a distinction between two types of target populations: general and special. General populations are usually defined by place of residence and age, for instance, residents of California over 18 years of age. Both the North Carolina Citizen Survey and the national household survey in the previous chapter are general population studies, as are polls such as the national Roper Poll or the Commonwealth Poll in Virginia.

In contrast, special populations, such as the elderly in Florida and the deinstitutionalized in Virginia, are more narrowly defined populations. Usually they are defined by the conditions of individuals or units that have theoretic significance or by policy statements about target populations.

GENERAL POPULATION SAMPLING FRAMES

As a rule, researchers find locating an available list of the general population difficult, if not impossible. On the national level, no list is available
of the general population. The general population is constantly changing
due to migration, deaths, and aging into adult status. However, a list is
sometimes available at the local level. An up-to-date city directory or a listing
of water or electrical connections will often be reasonably complete. A
researcher using either of these listings will omit new residences and the
homeless. The impact of these omissions must be considered in light of
the cost and completeness of the alternatives to using an existing list.

The first alternative is to compile a list from multiple sources. In the
North Carolina example, two lists were used to generate a more comprehensive list of the population. Using a list from tax returns and the list of
medical service eligibles, the researchers covered approximately 94% of
the households in the state. For localities, it may be possible to use lists
of personal property tax or local income taxpayers in combination with lists
of social service clients or eligible medical service clients.

Before using a combination of available lists, the researcher should
estimate the percentage of households or population that is not included
in the two lists after any duplication in the lists has been accounted for.
Also, it is important to attempt to define specific groups that the combined
lists are likely to omit. In some cases, another list could be identified that
would contain members of the previously omitted group of the population.
In other cases, poststratification—weighting of members of the under-
sampled group to give them proportional representation—may reduce the
problem. In any case, the problem should be reviewed and its impact in
terms of nonsampling bias and constraining the usefulness of the data should
be addressed before using the combination of lists approach.

A second set of alternatives is to use a technique that does not require
a sampling frame. Three often-used techniques do not require a sampling
frame: random digit dialing, cluster or multistage sampling, and systematic
sampling.

Random digit dialing requires the random generation of telephone
numbers that are subsequently used to obtain telephone interviews. The
Waksberg two-stage method of generating telephone numbers was used in
the study of the frail elderly in Florida. Random digit dialing removes the
nonsampling bias that occurs due to the omission of unlisted numbers and
new listings that occurs when using a telephone book for a sampling frame.
However, it excludes the portion of the population that does not have phones.

Furthermore, generally it can only be used in studies where telephone interviews are appropriate.

Cluster or multistage sampling is the second technique that does not require a sampling frame. A list of the members of the study population is only required at the final stage and only for the population members in the units selected in the stage immediately prior. For example, a four-stage sample of public school students could be designed with school districts as the primary sampling unit, schools as the secondary sampling unit, classrooms as the tertiary sampling unit, and students as the final sampling unit. At the first stage, a complete list of school districts would be needed. In the second stage, lists of schools would only be needed for the school districts actually selected in the first stage. Lists are only needed for the units selected in the immediately prior stage, thus reducing the effort to prepare the sampling frames.

For general population studies, area probability sampling is a form of multistage sampling that is often used because a comprehensive listing is unavailable. The national sample of households is an example of area probability sampling. Complete listings of the available sampling units are needed at each stage. In the selection of primary sampling units, a complete listing of Standard Metropolitan Statistical Areas (SMSAs), Standard Consolidated Areas (SCAs), and counties is required. But the listing of cities, towns, and rural areas is only needed for the primary sampling units actually selected in the first stage. Using personal interviews for data collection is tied to area probability sampling. Furthermore, this approach generally inflates the sampling error by 1.5 to 2 times the sampling error for simple random samples of the same size (Stuart, 1963).

Systematic sampling is the final technique that does not require a sampling frame. However, systematic sampling does require physical presence of the sampling units if a list is not used. Obviously, there are no practical applications of systematic sampling for general population studies. It is useful in special population studies where case files are available in local or district offices for clients, but no central list is compiled or it is not compiled on a timely basis. Also, it is useful for sampling invoices or other transactions that are not listed centrally.

Each of the alternatives for sampling frames have limitations that may make their use inappropriate in certain studies. If data must be collected in personal interviews, random digit dialing is not a viable option unless the geographic region in which the population is located is limited. The choice of a sampling frame or an alternative to a frame must be made considering the ramifications for data collection methods, cost, and total error. Both nonsampling bias and sampling variability can be affected by the choice that is made.

SPECIAL POPULATION SAMPLING FRAMES

In addition to the three approaches to obtaining a sampling frame for the general population (using an existing list, combining two or more existing lists, and using a technique that avoids the need for a list), a fourth alternative can be added, compiling a list. For small populations that are readily identifiable, it is possible to compile a list. For example, a list of school board members in a state can be compiled by requesting information from each school district. A list of museum visitors can be compiled from logs of visitors maintained at individual museums.

Researchers should avoid the trap of automatically using an existing list when designing a special population sample. Existing lists provide convenient sampling frames, but they may exclude significant parts of the population. This causes nonsampling bias in many cases. In the needs assessment of the elderly, using the existing list of clients for publicly provided medical and social services would exclude the elderly not receiving services and those who are receiving services from private sources.

Professional organizations and associations often maintain lists of members that tempt researchers to use them for sampling frames. This is a good option if the members are all in the target population and the target population does not contain any individuals that are not members of the organization. For example, using a list of members of a statewide teachers' organization would be appropriate for a study of the members of the organization. However, if the target population is all teachers in a state, nonmembers of the organization, who may be substantially different than organization members, would be omitted from the study.

Researchers should carefully evaluate any existing list for the nonsampling bias that is likely to arise, if the list is used for the sampling frame. Alternatives should be explored and evaluated in terms of their feasibility, cost, constraints on other choices, and total error. Feasibility poses the specific question, can the alternative be used? For example, random digit dialing is impractical when the target population is less than 10%-20% of the general population according to Lavrakas (1986).

In the Florida needs assessment for the elderly, the target population (6.5% of the general population) represented a minimum percentage to be surveyed using random digit dialing. The survey required nearly 72,000 phone calls to obtain 1,647 interviews. Despite the number of calls, the cost per completed interview was relatively low, $40 each, much lower than in-person interviews (Stutzman, 1985). In addition, using the alternative of random digit dialing makes any data collection method other than telephone interviews for all practical purposes infeasible. For the needs assessment, a study objective was to test the use of telephone interviews for surveys of this target population.

TOTAL ERROR AND SAMPLING FRAMES

Sampling frames can affect total error of the sample design. Specifically, sampling frames are one of the two major causes of nonsampling bias or the discrepancy between the target and study populations. Researchers should investigate the impact of four potential flaws of frames on total error before using them:

- Omissions: target population units missing from frame
- Duplications: units listed in frame more than once
- Ineligibles: units not in target population contained in frame
- Cluster listings: groupings of units listed in frame

Each of these flaws can contribute to nonsampling bias and, therefore, to the total error. These flaws are also present in the techniques that do not require actual listings of the target population. In addition, alternatives that do not require actual lists can add to total error by inflating the standard error due to the sampling technique used (cluster or multistage sampling).

Omissions. Omissions are members of the target population that are not included in the sampling frame. The national household survey omits residents of Alaska and Hawaii as well as those residing in institutions. These are known omissions. Estimates of the total number of households derived from the sample are 5%-6% below the U.S. Bureau of the Census estimates (Hess, 1985, p. 58). These are not completely accounted for by known omissions.

Omissions are discrepancies between the target population and the survey population. Therefore, omissions are sources of nonsampling bias. Omissions, by their nature, are the most intractable flaw of sample frames. Known omissions can often be corrected, if the bias they create is substantial enough to justify the cost. Alaskan and Hawaiian residents could be included in the national household survey. They are not included because of the cost of hiring and maintaining trained interviewers for such small portions of the general population of the nation.

Omissions that are not identifiable or unreachable are more difficult to eliminate, irrespective of cost. The sampling frame for the North Carolina citizen survey omits approximately 6% of the population. It is not obvious who the omitted residents are. Thus, it is not clear how the sampling frame could be improved. In cases such as this, the sampling frame must be evaluated against the alternatives, random digit dialing and area probability sampling.

The evaluation should rely on the four criteria: total error, cost, feasibility, and constraints on other study choices. Practical sampling decisions result from the evaluation of relevant alternatives, not from assessing the sampling frame against an ideal. However, the alternatives must include options that sufficiently limit the total error to a tolerable level, or the study results may not be usable. The tension between reducing error and increasing costs has led to creative solutions in sample design, such as the example of the study of homeless in Los Angeles (Burnam & Koegel, 1988), cited earlier. The strategy they employed was to enumerate all homeless persons and sample from within three strata: persons using temporary quarters to sleep, persons receiving meals but not beds, and persons congregating in indoor areas over the period of a month.

Duplications. When a member of the population appears on the sampling frame more than once, duplication occurs. Examples of duplication abound. Households with more than one phone line are duplicates for random digit dialing. Households with multiple listings in telephone directories are duplicates when the directory is used as the sampling frame. The overlap between the two lists used for the North Carolina citizen survey is a duplication problem.

The final example of duplication occurs when the sampling frame contains a list of transaction points rather than individuals. For example, the study of deinstitutionalized patients used a list of discharges from institutions as the sampling frame, which included duplicate listing of individuals. Releases are transaction points through which a single individual can pass several times. Multiple listings for a single individual on the list represents duplications. Because of the short time span over which discharges were placed on the sampling frame (two months), duplications were kept to a minimum for this study.

Duplications can be dealt with before the selection of the sample or after. Before sampling, duplicate listings can be purged from the sampling frame. For large populations, this procedure can be expensive and time consuming.

Alternatively, duplication can be compensated for after the sample is selected. Duplication can be viewed as increasing the probability of selection for the duplicated listing. The following listing provides a simple example:

Ike
Mary
Don
Miguel
Debbie
Assad
Juanita
Ike
Jimmy
LaFarn

The list of 10 names contains a duplicate; Ike is listed twice. Assume that three students are to be selected from the list. Juanita has a probability of .3 (3/10) or a 30% chance of being selected for the sample. Ike has a .3 probability of being selected for each listing or an overall selection probability of .6.

The sampling bias created by unequal probabilities of selection can be compensated for by weighting. In this case, the weight is the reciprocal of the number of times the name appears in the listing: 1/2 or .5. The weight compensates for the likelihood that twice as many individuals with two listings will appear in the overall sample as the proportion of the population that they represent. Failure to properly weight can have significant consequences. For example, the number of recidivists or individuals with multiple admissions to mental hospitals can be overestimated if the sample is drawn from a listing of patient releases and no adjustment is made for the probability of selecting individuals with multiple releases.

To determine the weights, the number of listings for each member of the sample must be determined. This involves a significant effort for large sampling frames and large samples. The effort is significantly reduced when the sampling frame is an automated listing with unique identification codes and the duplications can be determined by the computer. For the random digit dialing technique, a question must be added to the interview asking, How many phone lines are connected to this house? The number is then used as the denominator for weighting the responses.

Ineligibles. Ineligibles are units that appear on the list but are not members of the target population. Ineligibles in the North Carolina study could include individuals that have moved out of the state after the list was compiled but before the survey was conducted. Ineligibles in the study of the frail elderly are those households contacted with no resident over 75.

TABLE 5.1

Screen for Advanced Elderly

Starting Time: _____

Hello, my name is _____. I'm calling from the Florida State University in Tallahassee. Here at the university we are currently working on a survey concerning the service needs of residents 75 years of age or older.

First, I need to be sure I dialed the right number. Is this . . .

Since this number was randomly selected by a computer, I need to know if this is a home or a business.

Business — Thank you for your help. We are studying residences only, so we need not take any more of your time.

Home — Next question.

Does anyone 75 years old or older live in your household?

No — Thank you for your help. We are interviewing only people 75 years and older, so we need not take more of your time.

Yes — Next question.

The number of ineligibles appearing on a sampling frame should be minimized where possible. Attempting to collect data from ineligibles can drain resources from the collection of eligible respondents. Obviously, this is more costly with personal interviews than with telephone interviews. Ineligibles can be a significant problem for mailed surveys that require expensive and involved follow-up efforts to achieve satisfactory response rates. Furthermore, it is impossible to separate ineligible from eligible nonrespondents for an accurate computation of nonresponse.

When it is not possible to remove ineligibles from a list, the ineligibles must be screened effectively, but without removing eligibles. The screen used in the study of advanced elderly in Florida is shown in Table 5.1. This type of screen allows researchers to separate ineligibles from refusals in order to evaluate the potential bias from refusals. Often, in personal interviews and telephone interviews, a double test is used before the individual or household is screened from the survey. First, the respondent is asked to respond to a question or series of questions that the interviewer can use to assess the respondent's eligibility. If the interviewer judges the respondent ineligible, the respondent is asked directly whether or not she or, in many cases, any member of the household is in the target population. Obviously, mailed surveys can use only the respondent's judgment of eligibility.

The presence of ineligibles on a list does not bias the results unless eligibles are inadvertently screened out or ineligibles are included. However, they must be estimated in the design process and, as shown in Chapter 6, adjustments are made in the number of units selected from the sampling frame. For example, if 1,500 respondents are needed for the sample and the sampling frame contained 20% ineligibles, drawing 1,500 units would be expected to yield only 1,200 (1,500 × (1 − .2)) eligible respondents. To compensate, 1,875 (1,500 ÷ (1 − .2)) units should be selected from the listing.

Cluster listings. Many sampling frames are lists of groups of the units that are to be analyzed rather than the units themselves. General population surveys often use households as the sampling unit rather than individuals. This is the case in three examples presented in Chapter 4: the citizen survey, the study of the frail elderly, and the national household study. This phenomenon can be especially confusing when the household is the unit of analysis for some variables, and the individual is the unit of analysis for other variables. All three examples exhibit the use of alternate units of analysis, households for some variables and individuals for others.

The problem is not limited to sampling frames based on households. In policy studies, a case is often the sampling unit listed on the sampling frame. A case can be an individual or it can be several individuals grouped together as one case. For example, a social service agency may keep a listing of foster care cases. Cases may be defined as residents of a household providing foster care. The number of foster-care recipients as well as the number of adults and nonfoster-care children in the home may vary substantially.

Having clusters as listings poses two problems for the researcher: (1) choosing a respondent or respondents and (2) determining the probability of selection. When more than one eligible respondent is included in a single listing, all eligible respondents may be interviewed or one respondent may be selected. The study purpose will determine which is most useful. If all eligible respondents are selected, the sample should be considered a cluster sample.

Selection of one respondent can be done by stipulating the criteria for selection, such as the head of household or the oldest foster care recipient from the earlier examples. However, these methods bias the results when applied to individuals. Head of household criteria tend to oversample middle-aged males. Using whomever answers the door or the phone as the respondent also creates bias: "interviewer discretion, respondent discretion, and availability (which is related to working status, life-style, age) would affect who turned out to be the respondent" (Fowler, 1984, p. 33).

A preferable method of selection, originally developed by Kish (1965), randomizes the selection process. The process involves listing the eligible

TABLE 5.2
Troldahl-Carter Respondent Selection Matrix Example

Number of males	Number of Adults in Household			
	1	2	3	4 or more
0	Woman	Oldest woman	Youngest woman	Youngest woman
1	Man	Man	Man	Oldest woman
2	—	Oldest man	Youngest man	Youngest man
3	—	—	Youngest man	Oldest man
4 or more	—	—	—	Oldest man

respondents, numbering them consistently, and selecting a number that represents one individual from a random number table provided on the interview form. Again, this procedure is not applicable for mailed surveys.

Two methods have been proposed and evaluated as alternatives to the method proposed by Kish. When using the Kish method in telephone surveys, researchers felt that too much interviewer time was required, which led to refusals and, therefore, nonsampling bias. The Troldahl-Carter selection method was developed to shorten the process (1964). Only two questions are required to select a respondent for a general population sample:

- How many persons 18 years or older live in your household, including yourself?
- How many of them are men?

Based on the responses to those two questions, the interviewer selects a respondent based on a matrix of possible respondents. Four versions of the matrix are used in a general population study to balance the selection. An example matrix is shown in Table 5.2. This technique has a slightly biased sampling in that only the oldest or youngest of either gender are selected, leaving out the respondents in between. But this is only a problem in households with more than two adults of the same sex. Also, the technique usually results in an oversampling of females. In one study, the refusals attributable to the difference in selection or respondent technique were minimal: 7.8% for the Kish method; 7.2% for the Troldahl-Carter method (Czaja, Blair, & Sebestile, 1982).

The second method has been labeled the "most recent birthday" selection. For this method, one question is used to determine the respondent: "Of the people who currently live in your household, who are 18 or older, who had the *most recent* birthday?" O'Rourke and Blair (1983) found that only 1.8% of the interviews were terminated in the selection process using the most recent birthday selection; the Kish method produced 4.1% refusals. This technique, although systematic rather than random, produced no observable bias in the experiment.

Selecting one respondent from a cluster listing that contains only one eligible presents a different probability of selection than selecting one respondent from a listing that contains three eligibles. The probability of selection is three times as large in the first situation as in the second. Weights can be used to remove the bias caused by the unequal probabilities. An example of a similar weighting scheme was provided by the North Carolina study in the previous chapter: weights assigned are the reciprocal of the probability of selection. The weight of one is assigned in the case of one eligible; three is the weight in the case of three eligibles. A more complex method is shown in the example that adjusts the weighted sample size to equal the unweighted sample size.

CONCLUSIONS

Sampling frame decisions are the first step in the sample design after the presampling choices have been made. Three alternative approaches are available for sampling frames: (1) using an existing list, (2) combining lists or compiling a list, (3) using a technique that does not require a list. The choice of the frame designates the population to which the study results can be inferred. When the study population and the target population are synonymous, one source of nonsampling bias is eliminated. For practical reasons this level of agreement is nearly impossible. Therefore, sampling frame decisions are framed in terms of trade-offs. Effort spent in improving the sampling frame cannot be spent in reducing sampling variability, for example, increasing the sample size. Both contribute to total error, and the choice of which to expend resources on must be weighed in that light.

Furthermore, decisions about sampling frames often affect other choices for the research. For example, random digit dialing, for all practical purposes, constrains the researcher to the use of telephone interviews. Sampling frame choices should be considered in context with the other choices to be made in the design process. Alternatives should be compared weighing the cost of obtaining the sampling frame and collecting data using the frame, the feasibility of obtaining and using the frame, the total error (bias and variability), and implications for other study choices of using the frame.

The selection of a frame will often be done by informally examining the implications of one frame alternative, then another. Tentative decisions are reached based on assumptions about the other design choices such as the sampling technique and sample size. Assumptions are then analyzed as decisions concerning the sampling technique, for instance, are made. If assumptions do not prove to be reasonably accurate, the sampling frame decision may be revisited and the process of testing assumptions begun anew.

6

Sampling Techniques

Once researchers opt for a probability sample, they have five techniques from which to choose:

Simple random sampling
Systematic sampling
Stratified sampling
Cluster sampling
Multistage sampling

However, each technique actually requires myriad decisions for implementation. This is further complicated by the fact that combinations of the techniques are often used to reduce total error. For example, systematic selection can be used with cluster sampling to gain the benefits of proportional stratification if the clusters can be ordered using an important variable.

Once again, consideration must be given to total error, cost, feasibility, and implications for other choices when selecting a technique and an implementation strategy. Also, the choice of a sampling frame alternative will often constrain the choices for a sampling technique.

Prior to the decision about the technique, advantages of equal probability and unequal probability selection should be considered. Equal probability of selection guarantees all study population members an equal likelihood of being selected in the sample. The sample is selfweighting. For multistage samples, the overall probability of selection determines whether the probability of selection is equal.

Unequal probability of selection methods have known, but unequal, probabilities of selection for the members of the study population. Unequal probability methods require weights to correct for the bias that occurs from oversampling some groups in the population relative to other groups. Calculations become more difficult for estimates and sampling variability with unequal probabilities. For surveys where multiple data users are expected, the use of weights and appropriate calculations are a disadvantage for unequal probability of selection. However, unequal probabilities are often needed to improve the precision of an estimate or to allow reliable estimates of subpopulations.

In the examples, the study of the deinstitutionalized relied on equal probability of selection. There were no important subgroups that could be identified from lists available for sampling frames. Also, the data were to be analyzed by several individuals using a variety of techniques. Therefore, there were reasons to use equal probabilities. In contrast, the study of the frail elderly utilized unequal probabilities of selection to insure at least 100 interviews in each of the 11 service districts. Reasonably reliable regional estimates were needed and some less populous regions would have too few observations in the sample if equal probabilities of selection were used. Weights were applied to correct the bias from proportionately oversampling less populous districts. The cost of weighting was less than the benefit of regional estimates in this case.

Decisions about the probability of selection should be held firmly in mind when examining the trade-offs in the selection of a technique. The information required to choose and implement each technique, its advantages and disadvantages, and calculation of sampling variability is presented in the four sections that follow.

SIMPLE RANDOM SAMPLING

The most straightforward sampling technique is simple random sampling. Every member of the population has an equal probability of selection. In fact, each sample has an equal likelihood of being selected. Simple random sampling is used in situations where simplicity is the overriding concern and the advantages of other, more complex techniques, such as more precise estimates, are outweighed by the need for simplicity.

To select a simple random sample, researchers need a complete listing of the members of the study population. The sample can be selected by (1) assigning each member of the population a unique identification number, (2) selecting a random start in a table of random numbers, (3) using the number of digits in the random number table that is equal to the number of digits in the highest identification number, (4) selecting each population member that has a number that corresponds to the random number selected, (5) discarding any random number that does not have a corresponding number in the population, and (6) repeating the process until the desired number (n) of members have been selected. Figure 6.1 illustrates the process. For populations that have low numbers in the left digit—in the example 1 in 1,457—there will be many discarded random numbers. While this can be avoided with mathematical formulas, the simplicity of the process is sacrificed.

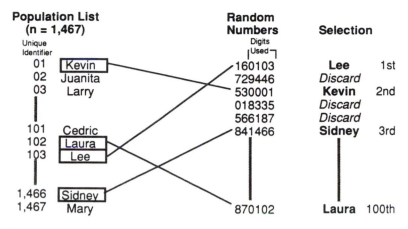

Figure 6.1. Using Random Numbers Table, $n = 100$

Many statistical software packages have a program that can be used to generate random numbers or actually select a simple random sample from an automated list. BASIC, the language used on most microcomputers, can be programmed easily to generate a series of (pseudo) random numbers tailored to the range of identification numbers in the population (Baker, 1988, p. 147). Many mainframe and personal computer software programs have a subroutine to generate a set of random numbers based on identification numbers.

The advantages of simple random sampling are the ease of selection and the ease of use of the data. Most standard statistical software assumes simple random sampling in the calculation of standard errors. Therefore, the programs are usable with no adjustments or recalculations. Once the sampling frame is assembled, no other information about the population is needed for sampling.

Disadvantages of this technique relate to the advantages of other techniques. It requires an explicit sampling frame, that is, a listing of the entire study population. If the data collection involves site visits or personal interviews, simple random sampling will disperse the visits across the geographic spread of the population. Travel costs are high, if the scope of the study is national or statewide. Finally, it is not as efficient, in terms of standard error per unit sampled, as techniques using stratified sampling.

Standard error formulas for means of continuous variables and binomial variables are shown below for simple random samples:

Standard Error of the Mean
$$s_{\bar{x}} = (1 - f)^{1/2} s/(n^{1/2})$$

Standard Error of a Proportion
$$s_p = (1 - f)^{1/2}((p)(1 - p)/n)^{1/2}$$

For both formulas, the finite population correction factor $(1 - f)^{1/2}$ can be omitted when the sampling fraction (f) is less than 5%. Example calculations of both formulas are given in Chapter 4.

SYSTEMATIC SAMPLING

Systematic sampling has statistical properties that are similar to simple random sampling. However, it can offer researchers benefits over simple random sampling in some cases. One of the benefits is the ease of selection in field settings.

A sample is selected systematically by: (1) determining the sample size, n; (2) determining the selection interval, i, where $i = N/n$ rounded down to an integer; (3) obtaining a listing or physical representation (files, invoices, etc.) of the study population; (4) selecting a random start between 1 and i to select the first member of the sample; (5) selecting each member of the population that appears at the random start plus a multiple of i, that is, $r + i, r + 2i, r + 3i, \ldots r + mi$, until the list is exhausted; (6) removing the number of units selected in (5) greater than n by a random selection process.

For example, in selecting invoices, a sample of 300 is determined to be needed from a population of 15,222. The interval is 50, rounded down from 50.74. A random start of 18 is selected from a table. Then the sample is pulled beginning with the 18th invoice, then the 68th invoice, then the 118th and so on through the population. Then, the number of sample members above the 300 required can be randomly removed. Selection of a sample in this manner has several advantages. First, a listing of the population is not necessary if a physical representation (e.g., files or invoices) is available. Second, the selection process does not require the use of a random number table or a random number generator in field settings. Relatively untrained staff can select the sample if given the interval and the starting number.

Another advantage is that systematic sampling can be used for de facto stratification to insure proportional representation of the population for some characteristic. To achieve de facto stratification, the units to be sampled must be arranged by the stratifying variable prior to the selection. Obviously, information on the stratifying variable must be available for the entire study population. The stratification variable can be either a continuous variable, such as the age of respondents used to order the population, or a discrete variable, such as grade level for a student. The variable is used to group the population to obtain proportional representation on the stratification variable.

In the deinstitutionalization study example, de facto stratification was utilized. The study was examining the transition from six public mental health hospitals to community-based treatment. By grouping the listing according to the hospital responsible for the release and selecting the sample systematically, proportional representation of the releases from the hospitals was achieved.

One caution is necessary in using systematic sampling. The sampling frame must be well mixed or purposefully arranged for stratification. If a cyclical arrangement of the frame is inadvertently used, the sample can be biased. For example, if the frame is a listing of monthly sales and six (6) is selected for the interval, only sales from 2 of the 12 months, say, March and September, would be included. Seasonal patterns would be ignored in the data and the results would be biased. This can be avoided by reducing the sampling interval to five in this case and removing additional cases as above.

If on-site fieldwork is required, a disadvantage of this technique is the dispersal of the fieldwork across the entire geographic spread of the study population. Costs of travel and supporting the fieldwork may be prohibitive. Formulas to compute standard errors for simple random samples can be used for systematic samples.

STRATIFIED SAMPLING

Stratified sampling involves grouping the study population into strata and selecting a random sample within each stratum. Stratified sampling is often used to ensure proportional representation for each stratum, decrease the sampling variability, or to yield a sufficient number of a subpopulation in the sample for reliable analysis.

Stratified sampling can be done proportionately or disproportionately. The former ensures proportionate representation of the strata by using the same sampling fraction in each stratum. Table 6.1 shows an example of a proportionally stratified sample. In the example, the level of mother's education is used to divide the students into three strata. This variable is known to be an important predictor of cognitive skills and, therefore, it is important proportionally to represent three groups: less than high school education, high school degree but no college degree, college degree.

TABLE 6.1
Proportionate Stratified Sample for Test Scores
Stratified by Mother's Education Level

	Stratum A1 less than high school diploma		*Student Scores* *Stratum A2* high school diploma; no college diploma		*Stratum A3* college diploma
1	96	1	120	1	121
2	103	2	107	2	132
3	113	3	99	3	154
4	91	4	127		
5	122	5	139		
6	107				
7	103				
n_h	7		5		3
$\bar{x}_h$	105.0		118.4		135.7
s_h	10.34		15.87		16.80
N_h/N	.467		.333		.200

n_h is the stratum sample size
$\bar{x}_h$ is the stratum mean
s_h is the stratum standard deviation
N_h/N is the weight based on stratum proportion

Proportional stratification. Because each stratum has different numbers of members, the samples for each stratum are different sizes when using proportional stratification, as shown in Table 6.1. For proportional stratification, the sampling fraction is the same for each stratum. The calculation of the mean, proportions, and other statistics uses the same formulas as simple random sampling, for example:

$$\bar{x} = \Sigma x_i/n$$

However, the calculation of the standard errors uses a different formula:

$$s_{\bar{x}} = [\Sigma(w_k^2 s_k^2/n)]^{\frac{1}{2}}$$

This formula adds the strata weight ($w_k = N_k/N$) to the computation of the standard error. For proportional stratification, n can be substituted for N in the formula. The formula weights the standard error for each stratum squared (s_k^2/n) by the relative population size of the stratum. Table 6.2 presents an example calculation using this formula.

TABLE 6.2
Standard Error Calculation for Stratified Sample:
Example of Proportional Stratification

	Mother's Education Stratum		
	A1	*A2*	*A3*
w_h	.467	.333	.200
s_h^2/n_h	15.29	50.36	94.11

$s_{\bar{x}}^2 = (.467)^2(15.29) + (.333)^2(50.36) + (.200)^2(94.11)$

$s_{\bar{x}}^2 = \quad 3.33 \quad + \quad 5.59 \quad + \quad 3.76$

$s_{\bar{x}}^2 = 12.69$

$s_{\bar{x}} = (12.69)^{1/2} = 3.56$

where w_h is the weight for each stratum (N_h/N),

$\quad s_h^2$ is the variance for the stratum,

$\quad n_h$ is the sample size for the stratum, and

$\quad s_{\bar{x}}$ is the overall standard error of the mean

Design Effect (Deff)

Standard error calculation assuming simple random sample

$\bar{x} \quad = 115.6$

$s \quad = 17.42$

$s_{\bar{x}}^2 \quad = 17.42^2/15 = 303.40/15 = 20.23$

$s_{\bar{x}} \quad = (20.23)^{1/2} = 4.50$

where $\bar{x}$ is the overall mean,

$\quad s$ is the standard deviation, and

$\quad s_{\bar{x}}$ is the simple random sample standard error of the mean

Design effect $= \dfrac{12.68}{20.23} = .63$

$(\text{deff})^{1/2} = \dfrac{3.56}{4.50} = .79$

Stratification reduces standard errors. this can be shown by calculating the standard error from the example ignoring the stratification and using the formula for simple random samples. The ratio of the stratified sample standard error to the simple random sample standard error is the square root of the design effect (deff), as calculated at the bottom of Table 6.2. For this example, the relative gain in precision is 21% (100 − 79). There is always a gain from stratification in terms of precision or reducing the standard error. The magnitude of the gain depends on two factors:

(1) *Variability Between Strata:* the greater the difference between the means of the strata and the overall means, the greater the gain; and

(2) *Homogeneity Within Stratum:* the greater the similarity within the stratum the greater the gain.

Kish (1965) explains this using the concept of the variance of the study variable explained (R^2) by the stratifying variable. The greater the explanatory power of the stratifying variable, the greater the gain from stratification. The gain is proportional to the amount of variance explained (R^2). In Table 6.3, an alternate stratification by classroom is used for the same population in Table 6.2. The 2% gain from this stratification, as shown by the square root of the design effect, is less than the gain from stratification by mother's education. The square root of the design effect for stratification by classroom is 98%, compared with 79% for stratification by mother's education. Mother's education explains more of the variance in student test scores than the classroom into which a student is assigned. Comparing the two examples, the range of strata means is larger for the mother's education stratification (30.7) than the range of means for the classroom stratification (16.0). Also, the variability or standard deviation (*s*) within each stratum is lower for the three mother's education strata.

Kish goes on to point out that the proportional size of the strata (*w*) has a bearing on the relative gain. Increasing the sample size for a small subpopulation, even though it is very different from the remainder of the population, will not improve the precision of the estimate significantly. Finally, the gains from stratification are generally small when percentages or proportions are the primary objective of analysis. Gains from stratification occur when the variability within the stratum is small (homogeneity) and differences between strata are large. Usually, it is difficult to stratify in such a way that the proportions between the strata are sufficiently different to improve the precision of the estimates.

The advantages of proportional stratification, as indicated above, are improving precision of estimates and insuring proportional representation of stratifying groups. Stratification does have a cost. Every member of the study population must be listed and categorized by the variables used for stratification. Obtaining this information on the entire population can be expensive. Sometimes it is less costly to obtain information for variables related to the desired stratifying variable. For example, it may not be cost effective to obtain information on mother's education for the entire student population. But information on the student's neighborhood, an indicator of socioeconomic status, may be available and that may be correlated with mother's education.

TABLE 6.3
Standard Error Calculation for Stratified Sample:
Alternate Proportional Stratification Example

| | Classroom Stratification | | |
	B1	B2	B3
	96	103	113
	107	120	99
	139	121	132
	127	103	154
	122	91	120
n_h	5	5	5
$\bar{x}_h$	118.2	107.6	123.6
s_h	16.90	12.76	20.77

$s_{\bar{x}}^2 = (.333)^2(57.14) + (.333)^2(32.56) + (.333)^2(86.26)$

$s_{\bar{x}}^2 = 19.55$

$s_{\bar{x}} = 4.42$

where $\bar{x}_h$ is the stratum mean,
s_h is the stratum standard deviation, and
$s_{\bar{x}}$ is the overall standard error of the mean

Design Effect (Deff)

Design Effect $= \dfrac{19.55}{20.23} = .97$

$(deff)^{\frac{1}{2}} = .98$

Disproportional stratification. Researchers facing situations where the overall sample precision is not sufficient or where the precision of a subpopulation is not sufficient, can turn to disproportional stratification. Disproportional stratification results from using different sampling fractions in different strata. Employing different sampling fractions causes unequal probabilities of selection and disproportional representation in the final sample. Thus, weighting is required to adjust for the selection bias.

The benefit from disproportional stratification results from lowering the sampling variability in one stratum where the standard deviation is relatively high by increasing the number of sampling units allocated to that stratum. The formula for standard error can be useful in understanding why this occurs.

$$s_{\bar{x}} = (\Sigma w_k^2 s_{\bar{x}k}^2)^{\frac{1}{2}} = (w_1^2 s_{\bar{x}1}^2 + w_2^2 s_{\bar{x}2}^2 + \ldots + w_h^2 s_{\bar{x}h}^2)^{\frac{1}{2}}$$

where $s_{\bar{x}k}$ is the standard error of the kth stratum, and
w_k is N_k/N.

This formula is the same as the formula for proportional stratification, shown above, except the standard errors for each stratum have already been computed in this formula. Either formula can be used for proportional or disproportional stratification.

Since standard errors are computed for each stratum and then combined as a weighted average, the strata with the largest standard errors and the largest weights have the most influence on the standard error. Increasing the sample size within the stratum that has the highest sampling error by disproportional stratification will reduce the sampling error within the stratum and, in turn, reduce the overall sampling error. Table 6.4 illustrates this case using disproportional stratification of the same strata as in the Table 6.2 and 6.3 examples. The reduction of the sampling error, as measured by the square root of the design effect, is approximately 2% less than the proportional stratification in each case. For example, the standard error for the efficient allocation of units for the mother's education stratification was 3.48, compared to a proportional allocation standard error of 3.56. The reduction is not particularly substantial in this case but the benefit is often greater when total sample sizes are larger than the $n = 15$ used in the examples.

To maximize the precision of the overall estimate of the population value, the sample size would be proportional to the standard deviation and size of the strata:

$$n_k = n(N_k S_k)/(\Sigma N_k S_k)$$

where n_k is the stratum sample size
n is the total sample size
N_k is the stratum size for the population, and
S_k is the stratum standard deviation.

While this formula seems logical, in practice the standard deviation of the population and strata are seldom known. Therefore, the allocation of sampling units to strata is imprecise, but results in improved precision when the standard deviations, or more usually their relative sizes, can be estimated. In the examples presented in Figure 6.5, 2 of the 15 sampling units were reallocated in the first case, 1 in the other. For the first example, stratum A1 was reduced by two and strata A2 and A3 receive an additional unit each. The second example decreased stratum B2 by one unit and added it to stratum B3. The variability of each stratum can be estimated by the same methods used in estimating the standard deviation for the efficient sample size: prior studies, pilot studies, using the range.

TABLE 6.4

Efficient Allocation of Sample Size by Strata:
Effect of Changing the Stratum Sample Size

	Mother's Education Stratum		
	A1	A2	A3
$\bar{x}_h$	105.0	118.4	135.7
s_h	10.34	15.87	16.80
n_h	5	6	4

$s_{\bar{x}} = 3.48$
$(\text{deff})^{\frac{1}{2}} = .77$

	Classroom Stratum		
	B1	B2	B3
$\bar{x}$	118.2	107.6	123.6
s_h	16.90	12.76	20.77
n_h	5	4	6

$s_{\bar{x}} = 4.34$
$(\text{deff})^{\frac{1}{2}} = .96$

where $\bar{x}_h$ is the stratum mean,
  s_h is the stratum standard deviation,
  n_h is the stratum size, and
  $s_{\bar{x}}$ is the overall standard error of the mean

Another use of disproportional sampling occurs when subpopulation analysis is needed, and the subpopulation sample size that results from proportional selection yields standard errors that are too high. Disproportional stratification allows increasing the sample size for the subpopulation without increasing the entire sample size proportionally. This necessitates that the strata be defined in such a way that the subpopulation members are associated with particular strata. The optimal stratification for this purpose occurs when strata are exclusively composed of subpopulation members. Strata where subpopulation members are in high concentrations can also be used with some loss of efficiency.

The central drawback in using disproportional stratification is the use of weights in the calculation of standard errors. The calculations become slightly more complex and the strata identification must be maintained in the coding and the resulting weights included as a variable on the data set. Many statistical software packages are set up to use weights in the calculation of population estimates and standard errors.

One of the most common errors in sampling occurs when disproportional sampling is utilized in the sample selection, but the population estimates are not adjusted for this bias because weights are omitted in the estimation process. Often this is the result of not integrating these two interrelated phases of the research plan, or having analysts unfamiliar with the sample design doing the data analysis. Weighting, using the design structure, is again discussed in the final chapter of this book.

Three of the sampling examples featured in Chapter 4 utilized stratified sampling. The national household survey used 74 strata in the first stage of selection. One primary sampling unit was selected from each stratum, with 10 of the strata composed of the 10 largest SMSAs that are selected with certainty. Designs using only one selection from each stratum create difficulties in the estimation of the standard errors. With only one unit in each stratum, it is difficult to estimate intrastrata variances. These designs require grouping most-similar strata together in the standard error computations.

The study of the frail elderly used the 11 regions of the state as strata. The study design called for a minimum allocation of 100 sampling units to each region and a total sample size approximating 1,500 units. The disproportionate allocation was done for two reasons: enhancing credibility of results within the districts and comparing between districts. Achieving this allocation increased the sample size for four regions and, therefore, decreased the proportional allocation for seven regions. For example, in district one, 113 completed interviews were treated as 33 interviews in the weighted estimates. Thus, by using weights, the 113 interviews were converted to represent 2.0% of the sample ($33/1,647 = .02$). (See Table 4.4).

The North Carolina citizen survey was originally conducted as a proportionally stratified sample. Each of the two listings used as frames comprised a stratum. The allocation of sampling units by stratum was based on the proportion of the population in each stratum. However, experience indicated that fewer of the individuals from the Medicaid list would respond than those on the tax return list. The proportion from each stratum were adjusted, from 11%-13.5% in the case of the Medicaid list, to produce a selfweighted actual sample.

CLUSTER SAMPLING

Cluster sampling is the random selection of groupings, referred to as clusters, from which all members are chosen for the sample. Cluster samples are useful when a listing of clusters is available, but a list of the population is not available. This often occurs when a program is operated out of several local or regional offices and a current, centralized client list is not maintained. Cluster sampling is also useful when the data collection involves site visits or obtaining records from regional or local offices. In these instances, cluster sampling can greatly reduce travel and training expense.

The trade-off that accompanies the economies of cluster sampling is the increase in standard errors due to the decrease in independent selections in the sample. Selection of each sampling unit in a simple random sample is independent of all other selections. For cluster samples, the selection of each cluster is random and, therefore, independent, but the selection of each sampling unit is not independent. That is, the sampling units included in the sample are determined by the selection of the clusters. This results in a loss of independence in selection. The loss of independent information from each sampling unit brings a loss in precision.

The impact of the loss of information is evident in the formula used to estimate the sampling error for cluster samples, in this case with approximately equal size clusters:

$$s_{\bar{x}} = [(1 - a/A)\ \Sigma(\bar{x}_a - \bar{x})^2/(a - 1)(a)]^{\frac{1}{2}}$$

where $s_{\bar{x}}$ is the standard error,
  a is the number of clusters selected,
  A is the total number of clusters in the population,
  $\bar{x}_a$ is a cluster mean, and
  $\bar{x}$ is the overall mean.

The number of clusters selected replaces the sample size, and the number of clusters in the population replaces the population size in the formula for simple random samples. This is because the number of clusters selected is the number of independent selections. Also, it should be noted that the deviation calculation, $(\bar{x}_a - \bar{x})^2$, is the deviation of the cluster means from the overall mean.

The first term in the formula is the finite population correction, which corrects the standard error for cluster samples when the number of clusters selected begins to exhaust the supply of clusters. An example of the calculation is shown in Table 6.5. The cluster means are 105.0, 118.4, and 123.4. The squared deviation of the cluster means from the overall mean (115.6) is 30.17. The square root of this number is 5.49. The calculation is also shown for the same sample assuming the sample was selected as a simple random sample. The design effect of using the cluster sample is approximately 1.49, which means that the standard error is inflated by the square root of that number, 1.22, over the standard error if the units had been drawn from a simple random sample.

TABLE 6.5
Standard Error Calculation for Cluster Samples

	Cluster 1	Cluster 2	Cluster 3
	96	120	103
	103	107	121
	113	99	107
	91	127	132
	122	139	154
$\bar{x}_a$	105.0	118.4	123.4

$\bar{x} = 115.6$

$s_{\bar{x}}^2 = \Sigma(x_a - x)^2/(a - 1)a$

$s_{\bar{x}}^2 = (105.0 - 115.6)^2 + (118.4 - 115.6)^2 + (126.0 - 115.6)^2$

$s_{\bar{x}}^2 = 30.17$

$s_{\bar{x}} = 5.49$

where $\bar{x}_a$ is a cluster mean,
  a is the number of clusters,
  $\bar{x}$ is the overall mean, and
  $s_{\bar{x}}$ is the overall standard error of the mean

Design Effect (Deff)
Standard error calculation assuming simple random sample

$\bar{x} = 115.6$

$s_{\bar{x}}^2 = 20.23$

$s_{\bar{x}} = 4.50$

Design Effect = 1.49

$(deff)^{1/2} = 1.22$

The size of the design effect depends on three factors:

Differences between the cluster means and the overall mean
Heterogeneity of the clusters
Number of clusters selected

The first two factors are closely interrelated. Standard errors increase as the differences between the cluster means and the overall mean increase. Sensitivity of the formula to the differences is increased because the differences are squared. Thus, the more the clusters differ, the less the precision.

Greater differences in means occur when the clusters are homogeneous. The design effect is 1, indicating the cluster sample has the same standard error as a simple random sample, when the standard deviation in each cluster equals the population standard deviation. The greater the within-cluster differences, the greater the sample precision. Finally, the number of clusters affects the precision of the sample estimates. This is analogous to the effect of increasing the sample size in simple random samples. Standard error varies as a function of the square root of the number of clusters. Increasing the number of clusters increases the precision of the sample. When using cluster sampling, selecting more clusters with less between-group variation improves precision. However, increasing the clusters can also increase costs of collecting data. The familiar trade-off between cost and precision is evident once again.

The impact of increasing the standard error from cluster sampling can be partially overcome by stratification. Conceptually, this occurs because combining the standard errors of weighted cluster means within strata improves sample precision. Stratification also improves the credibility of the sample by choosing clusters representing a variety of characteristics.

Geographic groupings and intact groups are commonly used for clusters. Counties are frequently used as clusters. Schools or, alternatively, classrooms are often used as clusters for education-related studies. Regional offices or local clinics are potential clusters for management or evaluation research. When clusters such as these are used, the researcher forgoes the opportunity to provide information on individual regions or schools, other than those units in the selected clusters. In the political environment, excluding some regions, for example, can undermine the credibility of the sample results.

MULTISTAGE SAMPLING

More frequently used than cluster sampling is multistage sampling, which has similar characteristics. A simple multistage sampling design, known as two-stage sampling, involves selection of clusters as a primary selection and then sampling members of the selected clusters to produce the final sample. More complex designs involve multiple sampling units selecting clusters nested within clusters, until the elements are selected. The national household survey is an example of multistage sampling.

The SRC national household survey employed five stages, six when individual-level data were sought. This survey was an example of area probability sampling of a general population. Each of the stages is defined by area. The first stage is either a metropolitan area or a county. Subsequent stages are progressively smaller areas: cities, towns, or rural areas selected in the second stage are selected from a list that includes all of the units comprising the selected primary sampling units. The process continues until one or more households are selected from a cluster that contains four households.

In this sample design, 74 primary sampling units are selected (one from each stratum) from the approximately 2,700 primary units that comprise the continental United States. On average, five secondary units are selected from each primary unit, which yields a total of 370 secondary units. The third and fourth stages lead to the selection of segments (units of four households) by first selecting blocks, or "chunks" in rural areas, then segments. The selection of the chunks and segments requires working with maps for each of the cities, towns, and rural areas. The secondary units are divided into clusters expected to contain 16 housing units. Then the clusters are divided into segments that are selected in the fourth stage. Households are the final sampling unit.

The principles that underlie multistage sampling are straightforward. However, execution of the design requires sampling expertise to avoid inadvertent biases. For example, if a cluster that is expected to contain 16 units is the site of the development of an apartment complex of 200 housing units, the sample could be biased unless the sample size is increased for the cluster, or the probability of selection is compensated for by weighting. Obviously, the decisions to be made in order to avoid bias and the supervision of the field operations to obtain the necessary information to make the decisions requires experience and expertise in area probability sampling.

A more tractable use of multistage sampling involves the selection of nested units to obtain a sample of special populations. For example, a researcher may need to select a sample of high school students to determine their attitudes about individuals of other races and cultures. In the first stage, school districts could be selected, stratifying by region, size, and location within a metropolitan area. For the second stage, homerooms within the selected divisions could be selected, including both vocational high schools and academic high schools. Finally, the students in the selected homerooms are selected as respondents for the survey (Figure 6.2).

Using this basic design, a researcher may choose either an equal or an unequal probability of selection, depending on the study objectives. To conduct subpopulation analysis on small segments of the population—for instance, minority students—a disproportionate sample with unequal probabilities would be useful. Alternatively, a common approach for an equal probability sample would be the selection of the primary units based on probability proportionate to size (PPS).

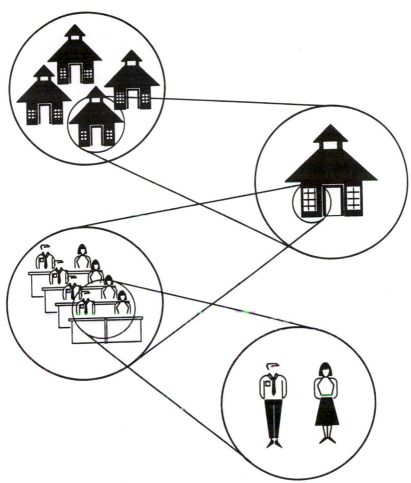

Figure 6.2. Multistage Sampling

To select districts based on PPS, a listing of districts, such as the one in Table 6.6, is needed, that includes a measure of size, in this case the number of high school students. First, the number of primary units must be selected. In this case travel restrictions limit the number of districts to 30. Then, a sampling interval is computed. The sampling interval is the total number of students divided by the number of units ($325,000/30 =$ 10,833). After selecting a random start (r) between 1 and 10,833, the primary unit containing the $r + 10,833u$ student is selected, where u equals 1 to 29.

Using Table 6.6, if a random start is selected of 7,278, the first unit selected would be Roanoke. The second unit would be the one with the cumulative number 7,278 + 10,833 = 18,111. Both Amherst and Nottoway would be skipped and Fairfax County selected as the second unit. Amelia, containing the 321,435th ((10,833 × 29) + 7,278) cumulative student, would be the last unit selected.

The probability of selection for any school district is $N_d/10,833$, where N_d is the size of the division. Combining this method of selection for the primary units with the selection of 5 homerooms and 10 students within each homeroom provides an overall probability of selection equal to .0045 for each student included in the sample. The extent to which the probabilities are exactly equal depends on the accuracy of the measure of size. The product of the number of homerooms times the number of students per homeroom must equal the number of high school students (measure of size). The total sample size is approximately 1,500 (30 × 5 × 10).

When using multistage sampling, the researcher may wish to preselect some primary units to be included in the sample. The researcher may want to insure that a major city is included, for example, Chicago in a sample of Illinois. In effect, school districts with more than 10,833 high school students such as Roanoke and Fairfax are selected with certainty in the example in Table 6.6. Also, the national household survey preselected 12 primary units for the sample.

To some this would seem to violate the principles of sampling. And, of course, selections with certainty (preselections) cannot be described as sampled units. But as long as the selections at the remaining stages produce probabilities equal to the probabilities of the other units selected in equal probability designs or are appropriately compensated for by weighting, preselections do not bias the sample. See the secondary primary unit selected in Table 6.6 for an example. The probability of selection in the first stage is equal to 1.07 (11,538/10,833), making the selection certain. A lower probability of selection in the final two stages (.0043) compensates for the preselection. Sudman provides an explanation and example of the use of PPS with multistage sampling when estimates of size for the target population are unavailable or inexact (1976, pp. 134-146).

Estimating the sampling variability for multistage samples is a complex process. Some commercially available software packages have subroutines that use Taylor series linearizations to estimate the sampling variability. For example, the Statistical Analysis System (SAS) has available subroutines to estimate sampling errors for a variety of statistics computed from complex sample designs (Holt, 1977; Shah, 1981). These methods require that more than one selection be made from each stratum in the primary selection and from each sampling unit at each stage. This can have the effect

TABLE 6.6
School District List for Probability Proportionate to Size (PPS) Sample

School	Students	Cumulative Students
Albemarle	2,318	2,318
Roanoke	11,538	13,856
Amherst	1,217	15,073
Nottoway	584	15,657
Fairfax	46,154	61,811
.	.	.
.	.	.
.	.	.
Amelia	3,121	324,071
Winchester	929	325,000
	325,000	

of decreasing the number of possible strata in the first stage by one half and therefore decrease the precision gains from stratification.

Another approach utilizes the concept of taking repeated samples and combining the results of the individual samples to yield the estimate of sampling variance. In this case, the sampling variability is computed by the following formula:

$$s_{\bar{x}} = [\Sigma(\bar{x}_i - \bar{x})^2/k\,(k - 1)]^{\frac{1}{2}}$$

where $s_{\bar{x}}$ is the estimate of the sampling error,
x_i is the subsample mean for the ith subsample,
x is the total sample mean, and
k is the number of subsamples.

However, the use of actual repeated samples, replications, limits the number of primary sampling units and therefore the number of strata that can be utilized. Thus, some precision is lost because of design inefficiencies. Furthermore, this problem increases when more replications are used. But the estimates of the sampling variability are less reliable if too few replications are used.

The method of balanced repeated replications was developed to overcome some of these difficulties. This method requires that two primary sampling units (PSUs) be selected from each stratum used in the design. For example, a design using 12 strata would require 24 primary sampling units. Each PSU within a stratum would be assigned either a + or −. A half sample would be selected using the primary sampling units indicated in row 1 of Table 6.7. Then its complement would be selected using the PSUs omitted in the first half sample. The sampling variance is estimated by

TABLE 6.7

Guide to Selection of Half Samples for Alternative Strata Sizes

Subsample	Strata Pair Selected											
	1	2	3	4	5	6	7	8	9	10	11	12
1	+	−	−	−	+	−	−	+	+	−	+	−
2	+	+	−	−	−	+	−	−	+	+	−	+
3	+	+	+	−	−	−	+	−	−	+	+	−
4	+	+	+	+	−	−	−	+	−	−	+	+
5	−	+	+	+	+	−	−	−	+	−	−	+
6	+	−	+	+	+	−	−	−	−	+	−	
7	−	+	−	+	+	+	+	−	−	−	+	−
8	+	−	+	−	+	+	+	+	−	−	−	+
9	+	+	−	+	−	+	+	+	+	−	−	−
10	−	+	+	−	+	−	+	+	+	+	−	−
11	−	−	+	+	−	+	−	+	+	+	+	−
12	+	−	−	+	+	−	+	−	+	+	+	+
13	−	+	−	−	+	+	−	+	−	+	+	+
14	−	−	+	−	−	+	+	−	+	−	+	+
15	−	−	−	+	−	−	+	+	−	+	−	+
16	−	−	−	−	−	−	−	−	−	−	−	−

NOTE: This table illustrates the selection of 1 member of the 12 stratum pairs to form a half sample. In each stratum (1-12), one member is assigned + and the other member of the stratum pair is assigned −. Sixteen subsamples are selected. In subsample 5, for instance, the − from the first stratum pair is selected along with the + from the second stratum pair, etc. The half sample selected in this way is then used to compute the statistic to be estimated (x, b, etc.) and then compared with its complement half sample. The complement half sample would include + from the first stratum pair and − from the second, etc. The results from computing the differences in the sixteen subsamples are then combined and the standard error estimated.

SOURCE: Frankel, 1971. Used by permission.

$$s_b = (\Sigma (b_r - b_c)^2/4K)^{1/2}$$

where b is the statistic being estimated
(mean, regression coefficient, etc.),
b_r is the replicate half-sample statistic,
b_c is the complement statistic, and
K is the number of replicates.

The simplicity of this calculation and its applicability to a variety of statistics often make it preferable to the Taylor approximations. However, it does require the calculation of separate estimates for twice the number of strata. Tables to guide the selection of half samples for alternative strata sizes, such as Table 6.7, can be found in Sudman (1976) and Frankel (1971).

The requirement to use balanced repeated replications for two PSUs from each stratum can be relaxed. When only one PSU is selected from a stratum, the strata can be combined to form strata with two PSUs. However, the combination of strata will be at the cost of an overestimate of the sampling variability. The amount of the overestimate may be insignificant.

The final method of estimating sampling variance from complex samples is the jackknife method. This method also involves repeated replications, but in this method, each replication computes the contribution of a single stratum to the sampling variance. The jackknife repeated replication method requires that from each stratum *at least* two PSUs are selected, but it is not *restricted* to two PSUs per stratum, as was the case for balanced repeated replications. For each replication, one PSU is removed and the other PSUs in the stratum are weighted to compensate, and the statistic is estimated. Then, assuming in this case two PSUs per stratum, a complement replication is computed by removing the other PSU in the stratum, weighting, and estimating the statistic. The individual stratum variance estimates are combined to estimate the overall sampling variability.

A number of important choices, as these calculations point out, remain after the choice to use multistage sampling is made. Most crucial is the choice of the number of strata and primary sampling units. The greater the number of strata and the higher the correlation between the stratification variable(s) and the variable of interest, the greater the precision of the sample. More strata require more replications. Thus, more strata will increase the complexity and cost of the computer calculations required. This cost is especially significant when maximum likelihood or iterative solution computer programs are being utilized. Too few strata will yield unreliable estimates of the sampling variable, however. Hess suggests that roughly between 30 and 50 strata work well for multistage samples using regression analysis (1985).

SUMMARY

The choice of a sampling technique depends on a variety of factors. Table 6.8 presents some of the most salient factors in reaching the decision about a sampling technique. Once a technique is tentatively selected, implications for field operations (including gaining access to records or respondents and developing sampling frames), nonsampling and sampling bias, and cost need to be thoroughly worked out. At that point, the sample size is the next concern to determine if the design will yield a tolerable error.

TABLE 6.8
Sampling Technique Selection

	Simple Random Sample (SRS)	Systematic	Stratified	Cluster	Multistage
Sampling Frame					
General	Random Digit Dialing (RDD)	Listing for small geographic region	Listing with stratifying variable for small geographic region	Geographic units	Area probability sample; Waksburg RDD
Special	Listing	Physical representation or listing	Listing with stratifying variables	Listing of clusters	Listing of primary sampling units
Data Collection	Telephone RDD; otherwise any	Any	Any; useful with different methods	Any; useful for personal interviews and record reviews	Personal interviews for area probability sample; telephone interviews/RDD; any otherwise
Benefits	Simple; self-weighting	Does not require listing for sample frame; pseudo-stratification	Improves efficiency; subpopulation analysis	Does not require element listing; concentrates travel time for personal interviews	Same as clusters but improves efficiency
Costs	——	——	Weighting needed if disproportionate, cost of information to stratify	Increases sampling error	Increases sampling error, computation of sampling error costly

7

Sample Size

As noted earlier, the number of units for the sample is usually the first question addressed by a study team to the sampling consultant. Response to the question must await information on other design and sampling choices. Why is the sample size important for a study? Sample size is the most potent method of achieving estimates that are sufficiently precise and reliable for policy decisions or scientific inquiry. The impact of increasing sample size on the estimates of the sampling variability is shown in Figure 7.1. The downward sloping curve indicates that sampling variability decreases as the sample size increases. However, the gain in precision is greater for each unit increase in the smaller sample size range than the larger sample size range.

Increasing sample size obviously has a cost. Larger samples require more expenditures for collecting data, especially when interviews are being utilized; following up on nonresponse; and coding and analyzing data. When increasing the sample size is done at the expense of effort invested in follow-up of nonrespondents, for instance, the total error may rise due to non-sampling bias. Choice of a sample size cannot be considered in a vacuum. Once again, trade-offs in cost, total error, and other design choices must be considered.

To begin the process of making a sample size choice, a number of factors must be examined sequentially. Prior to beginning the process, the determination of the tolerable error of the estimates or power of the analysis must be made. Policy studies, though they serve different purposes than studies oriented toward testing theory, are subject to the same criteria. The determination of tolerable error or power needs for a policy study tends to be defined more by the use for the information in the particular situation at hand than by conventional standards.

For policy studies, it is useful to involve policymakers in making the determinations about the precision required of the data. Their responses can be elicited by posing ''what if'' type questions, such as, ''Let's say the study estimates that 60% of the elderly are in need of services, but we are only reasonably confident that somewhere between 50% and 70% need services. Is the 20% gap too large for the information to be useful?'' or alternatively,

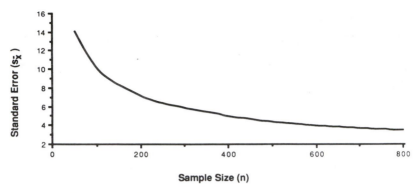

Figure 7.1. Relationship Between Sample Size and Standard Error

> You know that test scores of disadvantaged students are approximately at the 38th percentile on standardized tests. Considering the cost of this program and available alternatives, would you consider the program successful if scores were improved to the 40th percentile? How about the 43rd percentile?

Variations on these questions can be developed to fit the particular policy study. Cost estimates can be explicitly incorporated into the discussion to provide direct information about the relationship between cost and sampling variability.

The factors to be examined in the choice of sample size include:

Efficient sample size
Implications of the design for efficient sample size
Implications of the sample size and design for subpopulation analysis
Adjustments for ineligibles and nonresponse
Expense of the design given the sample size
Credibility

Each of these factors is discussed below.

EFFICIENT SAMPLE SIZE

Efficient sample size is based on an estimate of the sample size required to limit sampling variability to the desired level. For a study that is essentially descriptive, the sampling variability is set in terms of the level of precision needed for the estimates. Analytical studies use the size of the effect that the study estimates should be able to detect. Generally, efficient sample size estimates assume a simple random sample design, although with more information for studies that are frequently repeated, design-specific estimates can be developed.

The computation of efficient sample sizes for descriptive studies begins with the tolerable error (*te*): the standard error times the *t*-value for the selected confidence level. The variance or standard deviation of the variable must be estimated, also. Usually, the standard deviation can be estimated from a previous study. Some adjustment may be necessary if the target population for the study is different than the target population for the previous study.

Another method for estimating the standard deviation is the use of a small pilot study. Sometimes as few as 50 cases can provide a useful estimate. It is best to select the cases randomly from the target population, but this option is not always available. Judgment must be applied to determine whether the target population estimate would be expected to differ from the pilot study population. If so, an adjustment should be made.

A third method that obtains a rough estimate of the standard deviation can be obtained by dividing the range by four. If the highest and lowest value of a variable can be obtained from data or expert opinion, the estimate of the range can be plugged into the formula and the standard deviation estimated.

A final method of estimating the variance is often used when proportions are the statistics of interest. This method simply assumes the maximum variance that occurs when $p = .5$. The product of $p(1 - p)$ in this case is .25, the largest possible product of a proportion or a worst-case scenario.

The formulas for the efficient sample size for means and proportions are shown in Table 7.1 along with an example calculation for each.

In the first computation, the standard deviation is estimated to be 37.6. A tolerable error of 1.764 is used, which relates to a standard error of .9 units and a *t*-score of 1.96. The efficient sample size is 1,745 before the finite population correction (FPC) is applied, and 1,617 after. In the second example, the tolerable error of 2% yields a standard error of 1%. That is, the researchers will be 95% confident that the estimate of the proportion will fluctuate as much as 2% above or 2% below the true proportion. To obtain this level of precision, a sample size of 2,300 is needed after taking the FPC into account.

Even though these calculations are relatively straightforward, elementary statistics textbooks often present tables that give efficient sample sizes

TABLE 7.1
Efficient Sample Size for Means

$s = 37.6$ $N = 22,000$
$te = 1.764$ $t = 1.96$
$s_{\bar{x}} = te/t = .9$

$n' = (37.6)^2/(1.764/1.96)^2$
$n' = 1,745$
$n = 1,745/[1 + (1,745/22,000)]$
$n = 1,617$

 where: s is standard deviation estimate
    N is the population size
    te is the tolerable error
    t is the t-value for the desired confidence level
    $s_{\bar{x}}$ is the allowable standard error
    n' is the sample size without finite population correction
    n is the sample size with the finite population correction

---

Efficient Sample Size for Proportions

$p = .6$ $1 - p = .4$
$te = .02$ $N = 1,100,000$
$s_p = .01$ $t = 1.96$

$n' = (.6)(.4)/(.02/1.96)^2$
$n' = 2,305$
$n = 2.305/(1 + 2,305/1,100,000)$
$n = 2,300$

 where: p is a proportion of the sample
    te is the tolerable error
    N is the population size
    s_p is the standard error of the proportion
    n' is the sample size without the finite population correction
    n is the sample size with the finite population correction

---

and associated standard errors. These tables usually are based on the assumption that an estimate of a proportion is the objective of the study and that the maximum assumption for the proportion ($p = .5$) is appropriate. Also, a finite population correction is not applied. These tables fit a very limited number of situations and should be used with caution.

For analytical studies, efficient sample size calculations quickly exceed the capacity of this sampling text. Interested readers should begin with Lipsey (1989) in their quest for information on power analysis. An example of one study may adequately explain the concept of power analysis.

TABLE 7.2

Sample Size Needed to Detect Differences in Sentence Length

Sample size for each group (total sample size = $n \times 2$) n	Sentence length differences (months) $\bar{X}_B - \bar{X}_W$
30	16
50	12
75	10
115	8
295	5
775	3

where: n is the sample size for each group
x_B is the mean sentence length for blacks
x_W is the mean sentence length for whites

A study is to be undertaken to determine if differences exist between sentence lengths of whites and minorities convicted of the same crime. The study will analyze the differences between means of the samples of whites and blacks using the following formula:

$$t = \bar{x}_1 - \bar{x}_2/(s_{\bar{x}1}^2 + s_{\bar{x}2}^2)^{1/2}$$

For this study it is determined that the researchers will risk an error in finding a difference only 5 times out of 100 if no difference exists (i.e., $t = 1.96$).

Furthermore, the standard deviation of sentence lengths for rape of 32.3 months for minorities and 29.3 months for whites can be assumed from an earlier study. Finally, equal sample sizes are assumed in the calculation ($n_1 = n_2$). Using these assumptions, a sample size for each sample of 30 cases is needed to detect a 16-month difference in sentence lengths. However, if the sentence length difference is expected to be only 3 months, each sample would need 775 observations to detect the difference. Sample sizes required for various expected differences are shown in Table 7.2.

The estimates clearly show that smaller expected effects require larger samples to detect the effect. This relationship generalizes to other analytical statistics. The specific formula for the calculation of power can become quite complex. Lipsey (1989) provides an excellent reference for guiding a researcher through the factors that affect the sensitivity of a design to detect relationships. A sampling expert is often required to assist in the computations when power is the overriding concern.

IMPLICATIONS OF THE DESIGN
FOR SAMPLE SIZE

While sample size has the most direct impact on the efficient sample size, the design also has an impact. The efficient sample size calculations assume simple random samples. If the sample design deviates from simple random sampling, the efficient sample size is likely to vary also. Sampling variability increases when cluster sampling is used; it decreases when stratification is used.

The design effect (deff) is a direct way of addressing the impact of design on sampling variability. The design effect can be multiplied by the expected sampling variance ($s_{\bar{x}}^2$) in the calculation of an efficient sample size to adjust for the impact of the design. The design effect is the ratio of the sampling variance of the design to the sampling variance, assuming a simple random sample (Kish, 1965; Sudman, 1976). The square root of the design effect is used more often in practice to make it comparable to the standard error.

To incorporate the effect of the design into the calculation of the efficient sample size, information about the expected design effect is needed prior to the execution of the sample design. Naturally an estimate of the design effect is the best that a researcher can provide. For stratified samples, the design effect for means is likely to range from .5 to .95. The actual deff will depend on the number of strata and the correlation between the stratification variables and the variable studied.

Cluster samples can be expected to have a design effect greater than one. A common range would be 1.5 to 3.0. Obviously, a range of this size would have quite an impact on the efficient sample size. Determining the estimate of effect depends on characteristics of the particular design. The number of clusters, the homogeneity of the cluster members, and the use of stratification have an important bearing on the actual design effect.

Multistage samples, also, should be adjusted for design effects: "Sampling errors in multi-stage random samples are almost always larger than in unrestricted random sampling, and the effect of stratification at the first (and possibly later) stages is to reduce this excess but almost never to eliminate it" (Stuart, 1963, p. 89). Stuart offers a rough rule of a 1.25 to 1.50 increase in the sampling error. These numbers would be squared to multiple times the sample variance.

More recent work (Kish & Frankel, 1970; Frankel, 1971) gives the square root of the design effect for a variety of multistage samples and a variety of estimates. Two conclusions of Kish and Frankel are particularly relevant here: "Standard errors computed by machine programs, based on srs assumptions, were not gross underestimates [for multivariate analyses]";

TABLE 7.3

Sample Size and Subpopulation Analysis Analyzing 8 Equal-Size Districts

$n = 1,620$	$s = 37.6$	$s_x = .9$
$n_d = 1,620/8 = 203$		
$s_{d\bar{x}} = 37.6/(203)^2 = 2.64$		

where: n is entire sample size
n_d is sample size for each district
s is standard deviation estimate
s_x is standard error of the mean for full sample
$s_{d\bar{x}}$ is standard error for district subsample

and "Design effects were shown to be estimable and of appreciable magnitudes for standard errors of regression coefficients" (p. 1073).

In empirical investigations, the design effect was found to be larger for means than for regression coefficients. The rough guidance provided by Stuart (1963) proved reasonably accurate for the square root of the design effect for means. The square root of the design effect for regression coefficients tended to range from 1.06 to 1.30. Using the deff in formulas for efficient sample size can mean significant increases to the calculated sample size.

SUBPOPULATION ANALYSIS

Thus far, the consideration of sample size has assumed that the entire target population will be analyzed together. In many cases, subpopulations are of interest also. For example, in the frail elderly study a researcher may wish to single out females in the target population for a separate study. Another researcher may wish to analyze regions of the state separately. The subpopulation analyses have less precision than the analysis of the entire sample as a group. Fewer cases for the subpopulation increases sampling variability for the analysis by subpopulation, although smaller standard deviations for the subpopulation may offset the increase to some extent.

The impact of subpopulation analysis is shown in an example where program analysts are to estimate the length of time in weeks that cases have been open in a social service agency (Table 7.3). The efficient, full sample size is approximately 1,620. Conducting a subpopulation analysis of eight districts, where the districts are approximately equal size, would yield district subsamples of 203 units. The standard error of 2.64 for the district subsamples compares with a standard error of .9 for the entire sample. This standard error is 2.9 times the standard error for the total sample. The total size of the 95% confidence interval for the districts will be 10.3 (2.64 ×

1.96 × 2). If district estimates are important, the researchers must consider whether this confidence interval, ±5 weeks, is sufficiently precise for the purpose of the study. If not, the researcher must consider the cost of the total sample size necessary to increase the precision of each district to the tolerable error level.

ADJUSTMENTS FOR INELIGIBLES AND NONRESPONSE

In choosing the size of the sample, the researcher must remember that the precision of the sample is estimated by the number of target population members for whom data are actually obtained. Two reasons for not obtaining usable information for some of the sample selected are:

Ineligibles in the sampling frame
Nonresponse

Ineligibles include those listed on the sampling frame that are not members of the target population. Ineligibles contribute to increased sampling variability by lowering the actual sample size. For example, in the North Carolina Citizen Survey a resident of Virginia working and paying taxes in North Carolina could conceivably be included on taxpayer rolls. This individual would be ineligible for a poll of residents. Analogously, using random digit dialing for a special population survey will result in calls to many residences that do not contain a member of the target population and are screened out of the sample. The Florida study is an example.

Nonresponse occurs for a variety of reasons, including inability to contact the respondent and refusal to respond. Nonresponse can create nonsampling bias in the sample, because a portion of the population is underrepresented in the sample. Evaluation of potential nonresponse bias will be examined in the next chapter. Here an adjustment to the efficient sample size is offered to compensate for the impact of nonresponse on sampling variability.

Impacts from ineligibles and nonresponse can be compensated for by dividing the efficient sample size by the proportion of eligibles times the proportion of respondents. An efficient sample size of 1,620 will be adjusted to an initial sample size of approximately 2,006 when .95 of the sampling frame is estimated to be eligible and .85 of the sample are expected to respond.

$$n' = \frac{n}{(e)\,(r)}$$

$$n' = \frac{1620}{(.95)(.85)}$$

$$n' = 2006$$

where n' is the adjusted sample size,
$\quad\quad n$ is the efficient sample size,
$\quad\quad e$ is the proportion of eligibles on the list, and
$\quad\quad r$ is the proportion of respondents expected.

The higher the response rate the fewer the initial contacts that have to be made as a result of adjusting the sample size. Extensive follow-up procedures, while costly, have cost savings resulting from smaller initial sample sizes that can partially offset the additional costs.

EXPENSE

The cost of the data collection can be reasonably examined at this point. The examination should include costs arising from:

(1) obtaining the sampling frame, for instance, the cost of field operations needed to obtain housing site locations for area probability sampling

(2) obtaining and using information in the selection of the sample (stratification variables)

(3) data collection including initial contacts for the entire sample and collection costs of interviewing (travel, telephone charges, labor) or administering an instrument (mailing, travel, labor)

(4) follow-up procedures

(5) handling and coding completed instruments

(6) computer analysis

Except for the first two, these costs vary by the size of the sample selected or the number of responses obtained. Follow-up procedures are extremely important in the cost calculation. Investing in follow-up procedures can reduce the size of the sample selected by increasing the response rate, reduce costs associated with initial contacts, and eliminate the costs of nonresponse bias evaluation by reducing potential nonsampling bias. If, for example, the response rate in the example cited above could be increased from 85% to 95%, the adjusted sample size could be reduced from 2006 to 1795. The expenses associated with attempting to contact the additional 211 sample units, acquiring addresses or phone numbers, mailing questionnaires, calling for appointments, and so on, may be more than an intensive follow-up and reduce nonsampling bias.

CREDIBILITY

An efficient sample size is not always a credible sample size. Often users of information mistrust sample information that they perceive to be based on too few cases. Alternatively, the audience for the information may have a conception of differences across regions or unique local conditions that requires allocation of a larger sample.

Sometimes these concerns arise as a function of population size. Computation of an efficient sample size, as shown, has little to do with the size of the population. In fact, the population size is used only in the finite population correction factor. Yet the perception exists that sample size should be a percentage of the population size—often 10% is the figure used. This perception is not accurate. Sample sizes of 1,500 to 2,500 used in general population polls and voter surveys are common, although on occasion the question arises, how can 1,500 individuals speak for citizens in this country? Media use and accuracy of the polls have overcome much skepticism, perhaps too much.

Smaller sample sizes used for medical research and other studies of special populations are sometimes viewed with incredulity. Skepticism about sample credibility is exacerbated by departures from proportional allocation of the sampling units in the random selection process. Lack of proportional distribution of the sample, or in a more extreme case lack of representation of some legislative districts, may be grounds for dismissing the sample information in legislative policy-making. The fallacy of overreliance on the sample proportions mirroring population proportions is discussed Chapter 8.

For example, in an evaluation where a sample of 60 licensed homes for adults was selected for inspection and data collection, program administrators refused to accept the results. After a census inspection effort of over 400 homes, percentages of homes with problems differed by no more than 3% across several variables being observed.

Attacks on credibility of the sample cannot be eliminated in studies that have policy impacts. Prior planning and attention to factors that may serve to undermine sample credibility may thwart undue attacks. The researcher

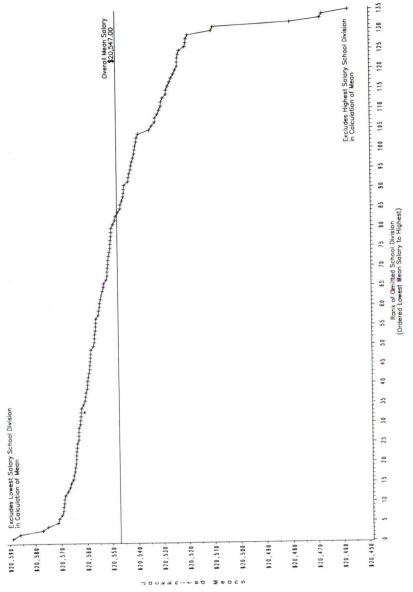

Figure 7.2. Sensitivity Curve for Means Using Jackknife Method

should ask questions of the audience for whom the results are intended, pertaining to sample characteristics arising from the design. Expressed concerns, such as sample size by region, may enable the researcher to alter the design to accommodate potential criticisms.

SAMPLING SMALL POPULATIONS

Frequently researchers confront the question of how large a sample to select from small populations. Populations such as counties, probation officers, or students enrolled in Latin courses are sometimes too large to allow data collection on the entire population due to resource constraints. However, potential sample sizes appear too small to produce reliable results. In these cases it is often necessary to consider certainty selections for target population members that must be represented for the sample to be credible. Results must be appropriately weighted to account for the probability of selection.

Another technique that can be used with small samples involves the analysis of outliers in the data. Small samples are particularly vulnerable to outliers. Outliers can unduly influence the estimates produced by the sample. The difficult question is when is an observation an outlier and when is it a reasonable representation of the population? Techniques for outlier identification and statistics that provide reliable, robust estimates have been developed in recent years (Andrews, Bickel, Hampel, Huber, Rogers, & Tukey, 1972; Barnett & Lewis, 1984).

One technique, jackknifing, is extremely useful and simple (Efron, 1982). Jackknifing involves the iterative removal of a single observation and calculation of the sample estimates, until each observation has been removed from the calculation one time. The estimates can then be ordered and plotted to show the sensitivity of the estimate to any single observation. Figure 7.2 shows the sensitivity of the mean for one sample. The sensitivity curve exhibits a range of 128 units, indicating a strong influence of the extreme values on the data.

SUMMARY

The selection of the sample size depends upon the amount of sampling variability that can be tolerated, the variability of important variables, the design effect, need for subpopulation analysis, ineligibles and nonresponse, cost, and credibility factors. These factors should be considered in combination when evaluating sample design alternatives. The formulas provided in this chapter allow the researcher to estimate the sample size needed when considering these factors.

8

Postsampling Choices

Completing the data collection does not eliminate sampling-related issues and choices. Three issues related to the sample design and execution require attention:

Use of weights
Evaluation of nonresponse
Presentation of the data

Each issue is discussed below.

USE OF WEIGHTS

Weights are usually required when the sample has not been selected with equal probability. Unequal probability of selection can produce sampling bias. It is, therefore, important to review each sampling choice made in the design to determine where selections have deviated from equal probability. Unequal probabilities can be caused by a variety of design features. A list developed from previous chapters includes:

Sampling frame duplications
Listing of clusters, for instance, households, on sampling frames
Disproportionate sampling techniques

It is useful to keep weights separate for each of the causes. In some instances, the use of a weight depends on the unit of analysis for a particular question.

Weights and the unit of analysis. In the North Carolina Citizen Survey, for example, weights were used to compensate for the selection of an individual from a household cluster. However, when the question pertained to the household rather than the individual, no weighting was necessary. Similarly, the sampling frame duplications for multiple discharges in the study of the deinstitutionalized caused unequal probabilities of selection when focusing on individual characteristics (e.g., number of times admitted to an institution). Questions asked about the discharge process were based on an equal probability selection of discharges. For example, a question about the proportion of discharges that involved community caseworkers in predischarge planning would not involve weighting.

Poststratification weights. Often weights are considered in order to make adjustments for deviations between the distribution of characteristics in the sample and the target population. This type of weighting is referred to as poststratification weighting. Differences between sample and census estimates of the North Carolina population are shown in Table 4.3. Differences in the proportion of males and females in the two are large enough to consider whether men are underrepresented. If the researcher determines the answer is yes, poststratification weights could be applied to the sample observations. The formula for these weights is:

$$w = p_p/p_s$$

where p_p is the population proportion, and
p_s is the sample proportion.

The formula can be used for univariate adjustments or based on the cell proportions from bi- or multivariate contingency tables for the target population, if available.

After the poststratification weights are applied, or any weights for that matter, the impact on the results should be analyzed. If the impact of the weights is negligible, they can reasonably be omitted, thereby simplifying the analysis.

Two further cautions should be applied before using poststratification weights. First, the accuracy of the population data should be considered. Population estimates initially available for the frail elderly in Florida were four-year-old census estimates. A discrepancy of over four percentage points between the census estimates of the percentage of elderly over 85 and the sample estimates were initially observed. In-migration of elderly into Florida or aging may have been responsible for a part of the difference. When the 1985 census projections were examined (Table 4.5), the discrepancy was reduced to 2.7%, within the expected range. No weights were needed to compensate for the discrepancy.

Second, poststratification is not a panacea for nonresponse. Rather, it is appropriately used to make weighting adjustments for the expected random discrepancies between sample and target population characteristics. Poststratification, used as a nonresponse adjustment, assumes that nonrespondents would have responded the same way as respondents with similar demographic characteristics. This assumption must be empirically justified. Nonrespondents are observably different than respondents in at least one way—they chose not to respond. Salience of the questions to individual respondents and availability of time during the survey period may be distinguishing characteristics that would affect responses. Nonresponse evaluation is the topic of the next section.

EVALUATION OF NONRESPONSE

Nonresponse creates a potential for nonsampling bias that cannot be overlooked after the data are collected. The effects of nonresponse bias can be substantial. The impact of nonresponse is analogous to the impact of omissions in the sampling frame, a portion of the target population has been omitted from the sample. The sample does not represent those individuals and therefore is not an accurate model of the population.

Kalton suggests that nonrespondents be considered a stratum for the purpose of evaluating their impact on the sample estimates (1983). The formula for stratified sample means in this case is:

$$\bar{x} = (n_r/n)(\bar{x}_r) + (n_n/n)(\bar{x}_n)$$

where n_r is the number of respondents, and
n_n is the number of nonrespondents.

Thus, the overall sample mean is the weighted average of the respondents' mean and the nonrespondents' mean.

Using the formula, a strategy can be developed for dealing with nonresponse. First, the best strategy begins with a plan to minimize nonresponse. The smaller the nonresponse proportion, the less impact nonrespondents have on the overall average. Plans for reducing nonresponse depend on the target population, the data collection method, and the funding that can be dedicated to this effort.

As is the case for most aspects of sampling design, developing plans for minimizing nonresponse should be done before the design is finalized. It may be worthwhile to select a smaller sample and use funds that would have gone into data collection efforts for more cases to reduce nonresponse. The deinstitutionalization researchers reduced nonresponse to 0.86% (3/350) by planning and implementing an intensive follow-up. While this is unrealistic for a general population sample, it shows the impact of intensive follow-up. Follow-up strategies and techniques can be found in many survey texts, including Fowler (1984), Lavrakas (1986), Dillman (1978), and Sudman and Bradburn (1982). Generally speaking, more personalized follow-up contacts are likely to garner a response.

After making the trade-off between initial sample size and intensity of follow-up procedures, a rather large potential for bias often remains. Nonresponse of 10%-20% can produce significant bias. A preferred method of evaluating the impact of the nonresponse is to obtain data on a sample of the nonrespondents. This involves randomly sampling the nonrespondent stratum and pursuing data collection through face-to-face contacts or over the phone.

The amount of data to be collected can be significantly pared down from the original instrument. To limit the data collection, variables of greatest interest and those on which the nonrespondents are suspected to be most different from the respondents should be selected. Analysis of the respondent stratum may provide information on dependent variables that appear to be important and predictor variables whose distribution may affect the overall estimates. The results from the sample can be used in the formula above to estimate the impact of the nonrespondents on the overall estimates. Sampling errors should be computed using the formulas for stratified samples.

A sample study of nonrespondents should be a complement to the follow-up strategy, not a substitute for it. The first priority in handling nonresponse is to minimize it. Allowing nonresponse to occur without attempting to minimize it causes total error to exacerbate due to the larger confidence interval bounding a biased estimate. Sample size adjustments for nonresponse, presented in the earlier chapter, only correct for one component of total error, sampling variability.

When a study of a sample of nonrespondents is impossible due to time and resource constraints, two methods can be used to inform the researcher of the potential impact of nonresponse. First, differences in patterns of responses from the first responses received to the next group to the final group can be analyzed. No differences between the "waves" of responses can indicate that nonresponse bias is less likely. This assumes that late responders may share characteristics with nonresponders. If differences do occur, responses in the last wave can be used in the formula for the weighted mean to estimate the nonresponse group.

A final method for evaluating the impact of nonresponse is to use the stratum weighted average formula to determine the pattern of responses that nonrespondents would have to exhibit to reverse the study conclusions. The formula can be rewritten as:

$$\bar{x}_n = (\bar{x}_c - n_r/n(\bar{x}_r)) \, n/n_n$$

> where $\bar{x}_n$ is the mean of the nonresponse strata necessary
>   to reverse the conclusion, and
> $\bar{x}_c$ is the overall mean that would reverse the conclusion.

For example, on a test where respondents scored an average of 94 out of 100 points, it was determined that a threshold (overall average) score of 88 was sufficient to show improvement. If a 90% response rate was obtained, an average score of 34 by the nonrespondents would be necessary to reverse the conclusions. Decreasing the response rate to 80%, an average score of 64 would change the conclusion. A 75% response rate would require the average score of 70 to change the conclusion, which could be well within the range of reason depending on the distribution of the scores.

Nonresponse considered thus far does not specifically deal with the problem of refusal to respond to a specific item, where other information about the respondent is obtained. This problem is quite different. Techniques for inferring values from information obtained are referred to as imputation. A variety of imputation methods, including the "hot deck" method and regression techniques are available (Kalton & Kasprzyk, 1982).

PRESENTATION OF THE DATA

This section is not so much concerned with technical report writing as with an accurate representation of the sample information. Recently, improvements have occurred in general reporting of sample information to lay audiences and the public. Newspapers and television broadcasts often contain a sentence that refers to the "margin of error" in poll results. The width of one side of the confidence interval ($\pm t(s_{\bar{x}})$) seems to be commonly used in these reports, although in some cases the standard errors are reported. The public has begun to comprehend the concept of sampling variability or at least in many cases has the information to consider it when digesting the information from the poll. However, the other components of error are seldom discussed.

This parallels many report presentations. Point estimates are often presented without a discussion of the total error. Standard errors are contained in a table or implicitly presented in tests of significance. Frequently, potential biases are not discussed.

Using information implies a risk. The risk is that the information may turn out to be inaccurate. In theory testing, scientists must determine whether the data provide a sufficient test of theory to move to other inquiries in the field. Clear presentation of the sampling choices made in the research should be adequate for other trained researchers to determine the validity and reliability of the information.

Policymakers also incur risks in using information. Program personnel, administrators, and elected officials may not be as well prepared to understand the risks. For these audiences presentation must go beyond recounting the choices made in the design and execution of the sample. The presentation must also be moved from the technical appendix to the executive summary. Facts as well as judgments are required in the presentation.

Each components of total error must be discussed in the presentation, not in theory, but in terms of its implications for the results. Since not all the implications can be quantified, judgment of the researcher must come into play. Differences between the target population and the study population, nonresponse, and standard errors should be discussed. Negligible biases from sampling bias or other sources should be reserved for more technical discussions.

Researchers should adopt the viewpoint of the audience in deciding whether and how potential error should be presented. If the potential error would likely alter the results of actions that the audience would undertake, they should be given the information to assess the risk. It is often difficult to determine the level of information to be provided and even more difficult to present it meaningfully to a lay audience. Graphs with ranges for confidence intervals and discussions that present estimates in terms of ranges are useful to convey the sense of sampling variability. The potential impact of bias, based on the results of the analysis presented earlier in the chapter, should be presented in the discussion of the study findings as a precautionary note.

In the final analysis, the level of information that researchers provide the audience determines the responsibility for the risk. When the audience is given sufficient information to assess the risk in using the results, they incur responsibility for the use of the information. When the uncertainty of study results are not reasonably brought forward, the researcher bears a share of the responsibility.

CONCLUSIONS

Practical sampling design is important throughout the study design, execution, analysis, and reporting. Choices made at one point in the study impact on later choices and procedures. Explicitly integrating sampling choices into the research process can usefully focus attention on total error. Reducing overall error, within resource constraints, is the objective for practical sampling design.

Total error is comprised of three component parts: nonsampling bias, sampling bias, and sampling variability. Each affects the accuracy of the study results. Design choices, such as selecting the sampling frame or choosing the sample size, directly affect the amount of total error. Evaluation procedures, such as nonrespondent sample studies or computation of standard errors, provide important information on the actual error in the sample findings. Researchers should assist consumers in assessing both the accuracy of their findings and the risks involved in using them.

REFERENCES

Andrews, D. F., Bickel, P. J., Hampel, F. R., Huber, P. J., Rogers, W. H., & Tukey, J. W. (1972). *Robust estimates of location: Survey and advances.* Princeton, NJ: Princeton University Press.

Baker, T. L. (1988). *Doing social research.* New York: McGraw-Hill.

Barnett, V., & Lewis, T. (1984). *Outliers in statistical data.* (2nd ed.). New York: John Wiley.

Bradburn, N. A., & Sudman, S. (1980). *Improving interview methods and questionnaire design.* San Francisco: Jossey-Bass.

Burnam, M. A., & Koegel, P. (1988). Methodology for obtaining a representative sample of homeless persons: The Los Angeles skid row study. *Evaluation Review, 12,* 117-152.

Campbell, D. T., & Stanley, J. C. (1963). *Experimental and quasi-experimental design for research.* Chicago: Rand-McNally.

Cook, D. C., & Campbell, D. T. (1979). *Quasi-experimentation: Design and analysis issues for field settings.* Boston: Houghton Mifflin.

Czaja, R., Blair, J., & Sebestik, J. P. (1982). Respondent selection in a telephone survey: A comparison of three techniques. *Journal of Marketing Research, 21,* 381-385.

Dillman, D. A. (1978). *Mail and telephone surveys: The total design method.* New York: John Wiley.

Dillman, D. A., & Tarnai, J. (1988). Administrative issues in mixed mode surveys. In P. M. Groves, P. P. Biemer, L. E. Lyberg, J. T. Massey, & W. L. Nicholls (Eds.), *Telephone survey methodology* (pp. 509-528). New York: John Wiley.

Efron, B. (1982). *The jackknife, the bootstrap and other resampling plans.* Philadelphia: Society for Industrial and Applied Mathematics.

Fowler, F. J., Jr. (1984). *Survey research methods.* Beverly Hills, CA: Sage.

Frankel, M. R. (1971). *Inference from survey samples: An empirical investigation.* University of Michigan, Institute for Social Research, Ann Arbor.

Grizzle, G. A. (1977). *North Carolina Citizen Survey, 2: How the survey was conducted and what it cost.* Raleigh: Office of State Budget and Management.

Hess, I. (1985). *Sampling for social research surveys 1947-1980.* Ann Arbor: University of Michigan.

Holt, M. M. (1977). *SURREGR: Standard errors of regression coefficients from sample survey data.* Research Triangle Park, NC: Research Triangle Institute.

Joint Legislative Audit and Review Commission. (1979). *Deinstitutionalization and community services.* Richmond: Virginia General Assembly.

Joint Legislative Audit and Review Commission. (1986). *Deinstitutionalization and community services.* Richmond: Virginia General Assembly.

Kalton, G. (1983). *Introduction to survey sampling.* Beverly Hills, CA: Sage.

Kalton, G. Unpublished manuscript, 1986. *Models in the practice of survey sampling.* University of Michigan, Institute for Social Research, Ann Arbor.

Kalton, G., & Kasprzyk, D. (1982). Computing for missing survey responses. *Proceedings of the Section on Survey Research Methods.* American Statistical Association, 22-31.

Kish, L. (1965). *Survey sampling.* New York: John Wiley.

Kish, L., & Frankel, M. R. (1970). Balanced repeated replications for standard errors. *Journal of the American Statistical Association, 65,* 1071-1094.

Kraemer, C. H., & Thiemann, S. (1987). *How many subjects? Statistical power analysis in research.* Newbury Park, CA: Sage.

Lavrakas, P. (1986). *Telephone surveys.* Newbury Park, CA: Sage.

Lipsey, M. W. (1989). *Design sensitivity: Statistical power for experimental research.* Newbury Park, CA: Sage.

Mark, H., & Workman, J., Jr. (1987). Populations and samples: The meaning of "statistics." *Spectroscopy, 2* 47-49.

McKean, K. (1987, January). The orderly pursuit of pure disorder. *Discover,* 72-81.

Oakes, M. (1986). *Statistical inference: A commentary for the social and behavioral sciences.* New York: John Wiley.

Office of State Budget and Management. (1982). *North Carolina citizen survey: Highlights 1981.* Raleigh: Office of State Budget and Management.

Office of State Budget and Management. (1983). *North Carolina citizen survey: Highlights 1982.* Raleigh, NC: Office of State Budget and Management.

O'Rourke, D., & Blair, J. (1983). Improving random respondent selection in telephone surveys. *Journal of Marketing Research, 20,* 428-432.

Raj, D. (1972). *The design of sample surveys.* New York: McGraw-Hill.

Rog, D. J., & Henry, G. T. (1986). *A community profile of the deinstitutionalized.* Unpublished manuscript, American Psychological Association.

Rossi, P. H., Wright, S. D., Fisher, G. A., & Willis, G. (1987). The urban homeless: Estimating composition and size. *Science, 235,* 1336-1341.

Shah, B. V. (1981). *SESUDAAN: Standard errors programs for computing of standardized rates from sample survey data.* Research Triangle Park, NC: Research Triangle Institute.

Skidmore, F. (1983). *Overview of the Seattle-Denver income maintenance experiment: Final report.* Washington, DC: Government Printing Office.

Smith, T. M. F. (1976). The foundations of survey sampling: A review. *Journal of the Royal Statistical Society, 139,* 183-204.

Stuart, A. (1963). Standard errors for percentages. *Applied Statistics, 12,* 87-101.

Stuart, A. (1984). *The ideas of sampling.* New York: Oxford University Press.

Sudman, S. (1966). Probability sampling with quotas. *Journal of the American Statistical Association, 61,* 749-771.

Sudman, S. (1976). *Applied sampling.* New York: Academic Press.

Sudman, S., & Bradburn, N. M. (1982). *Asking questions.* San Francisco: Jossey-Bass.

Stutzman, M. (1985). *Florida's 75+ population: A baseline data sourcebook.* Tallahassee: Florida State University.

Troldahl, V. C., & Carter, R. E. (1984). Random selection of respondents within households in phone surveys. *Journal of Marketing Research, 1,* 71-76.

Waksberg, J. (1978). Sampling methods for random digit dialing. *Journal of the American Statistical Association, 73,* 40-46.

Williams, J. A., Jr. (1982a). *North Carolina citizen survey: Overview, Fall 1981.* Raleigh, NC: Office of State Budget and Management.

Williams, J. A., Jr. (1982b). *North Carolina citizen survey: Technical report, Fall 1982.* Raleigh, NC: Office of State Budget and Management.

About the Author

GARY T. HENRY is Associate Professor of Public Administration at Virginia Commonwealth University. He teaches research methods and statistics, program evaluation, and policy analysis. Currently, he is the principal investigator for a project to develop and implement a system of performance indicators for all public schools in Virginia. He is affiliated with the Institute for Statistics and recently served as a Visiting Professor at Huangehe University in the Peoples Republic of China. Dr. Henry is a faculty member and a frequent lecturer for the National Conference of State Legislatures.

After receiving a doctorate from the University of Wisconsin, he worked for the Joint Legislative Audit and Review Commission in Virginia as Chief Methodologist. There, he applied quantitative methods to the study of eduation, corrections, and transportation. Subsequently, he served in the governor's cabinet as the Deputy Secretary of Education.

His research interests include robust estimation, assessing causal relationships in field settings, and evaluating equity. Dr. Henry is active in publishing and reviewing for journals such as *Evaluation Review* and *Public Administration Review* and serves as the Chairman of the Standards and Ethics Committee of the American Evaluation Association.

NOTES

NOTES

NOTES

NOTES

NOTES